Notebooks of a Chile Verde Smuggler

Camino del Sol   A Latina and Latino Literary Series

Notebooks of a Chile Verde Smuggler

Juan Felipe Herrera

The University of Arizona Press   Tucson

The University of Arizona Press

© 2002 Juan Felipe Herrera

All rights reserved

Manufactured in the United States of America

First Printing

07   06   05   04   03   02   6   5   4   3   2   1

Some of these texts have appeared in *The Americas Review; The Bayou Review;*
Chelsea; The Colorado Review; Currents Beneath the Dancing River Anthology;
El Andar; MSNBC.Com; Reclaiming San Francisco: History, Politics and Culture;
POG; and *The University of Arizona Poetry Center Newsletter.*

Library of Congress Cataloging-in-Publication Data

Herrera, Juan Felipe.
    Notebooks of a chile verde smuggler/Juan Felipe Herrera.
        p. cm.
    ISBN 0-8165-2215-4 (pbk. : alk. paper)
        1. Herrera, Juan Felipe 2. Poets, American—20th century—Biography.
3. Mexican American poets—Biography. 4. Mexican Americans—Poetry.
I. Title.
    PS3558.E74 Z4695 2002
    811'.54—dc21   2001003289

British Library Cataloguing-in-Publication Data
A catalogue record for this book is available from the British Library.

Publication of this book is made possible in part by the proceeds of a permanent
endowment created with the assistance of a Challenge Grant from the National
Endowment for the Humanities, a federal agency.

For my tío Jeno Quintana, who started the wave
al Norte, back in 1918, RIP, & for Bobby
"Zero Down" Páramo & Rosita
"Milagritos" Quintana

Tío Jeno, Parral, Chihuahua, Mexico, c. 1919

René, Juanito, Rudy, and Sonny, Escondido, California, 1955

Moment after moment, completely devote yourself to listening to your inner voice.—Shunryu Suzuki

This corrido was written under the influence of frijol juice, epazote and raw huevo combinations, eighteen ponchis con canela, abuelita Sofía's 300 buñuelos—direct from El Paso, a true Chicana care-package, machaca blues burros at Logan Heights cantina, La Bamba, Tijuana tortas de lomo, pierna y sesos con ceboya, also, two litros de jamaica, a bote of tepache and dos galones de orchata to wash it down, plus, for the road, seven double-breasted tacos, fritos, Indian style, al pastor, al sacate, al mojo de ajo and al viento, outside, leaning on an Oxnard Taco troka, in a mid-night route to Fowler, for a menudazo, after misa de Gallo and a sweat to burn out los malos fluidos, jechizos and chinches from the eskeleto, not to mention a manojo of fresh pan dulce and a champurrado with a tiny shot of anís del Mono for the clear feeling and finally a cilantro hair-spray after a mole-facial scrub and verdolaga shampoo.

—Conchita de la Dos Fridas
"Tus Tacos," Paisano Drive, El Paso, Texas

Everywhere is where followers of the way tune their minds.
Everywhere is not everywhere; it is called everywhere.—Hui-K'ung

Last time we saw this José, he was scamming tourists with friendship bracelets in Tecate.—La Migra, Calexico, California

Mercado

Acknowledgments

La Maga, Queen of Spices & Segundo Barrio Verde

Mamá Lola and Abuelita Sofía, Las Meras Meras on Alma School Street

Roberto Robles Sr., Jefe de la Salsa, RIP

My Jefitos, Felipe Emilio & Lucha Andrea, Advisors of the Perejil, RIP

Jimmy, Arlene Biala & Francis Wong—Singers of Red Chile

Glenn Horiuchi, Mochi & Ebony Master, RIP

Chente, Alvina & Tito, Judy, Grace, Julieta & Beto, Primos de la Olla Central

Las Cuatro Milpas, Logan Avenue, San Diego, 1958, Nati & Petra, Fire Starters of
    the Comalera, RIP

Alejo Quintana, Cousin of the Early Tortillas, RIP

Tío Beto Quintana, Pioneer of the Cantinflas & Tin Tan Dish, RIP

Joe Castel, Club 120 Go-Go Box Twister of the Snow Offramps

Tíos Chente, Jeno, Fernando and Tía Lela, Walkers of the First Pimientas, RIP

George Barlow, Bobbi, Erin and Mark, Doctors of the Inner Musics

Los Manis, Shamans of Cilantro and Sage

Demetria Martínez, Scribe of the Tránsito Internacional Guavas

Calaca Press, Ninja of Logan Nixtamal

Almasol, Joaquín, Joshua, Marlene, Roberto, Wizards of Canela & Papaya

P. Hartmann, Judith Allen, Christine Szuter, A. Otáñez, J. Franscendese, S.
    Kessler, R. González, V. Hernández-Cruz, I. Reed, L. Flores, Harriet Rohmer,
    David Shecter, L. Ferlinghetti, E. Katzenberger, Q. Troupe & N. J. Peters,
    Technicians of El Molcajete

Laura Tohe, Walker of the Medicines

Tim Hernández, Mike Medrano, Stela Molina, David Herrera & Diana Sevilla,
    Runners of Mad Grapeola

Alurista, Full Lotus Brother of Pluma Roja

Carlos Fuentes, Smoother of Thyme & Tiempo

Li-Young Lee, Mixer of Om-Fire & Garlic

Marvin Bell, Hat-Man of Jalapeño

Erik, Kathy, Pam, Little Randy (Rachel), Endsley III, John, Co-Weavers of
   Jellyvisions
Juan Carrillo & Tere Romo, Chefs of the Califas Alcachofa
Gerald Stern, Runner of Orpheus & Fried Chicken
Roberto "Jamulie" Álvarez, & Karen, Luis & Amalia, Keepers of Baja
   Trapiche & the Verdulera
Carmen Cristina Moreno & Daniela López, Warriors of the Valley Vines
Alfred Arteaga, Boatman of Glyph & Kelp
Carol de la Torre, Mambera of the New
Alison Deming, Twiner of the Shoo Bop West Marmalades
Mark Eades, Scribe of Merengue
Virgil Suárez, Epicure of Palma Light
Alma Flor Ada, Cumbia inker of Daily Planetas
Culture Clash, Pupuseros of the Piquant
Shin Lee, Seer of Habanero
Fernando Alegría & Tomás Ybarra-Frausto, Originators of Palta Alta & Bajo
   Sexto
Renato Rosaldo, Mary Pratt & Olivia, Rhymers of Tuksonian Guineos
Tede Matthews, Steve Abbot, Karen Brodine, Zooters of the Curry, RIP
Artemio Rodríguez, Etcher of Habichuela
Wanda Coleman, Tornado Catcher of the Buddhic Flow
Los Delicados, Shimmy-Dog Swishers of the Book of Arroz
Chitra Divakaruni, Knower of the Spice Shoppe Principles
José Cuellar & the Rockin' Jalapos, Movers of the Solar Accordion
Roberto Sifuentes & Laura Ayala, Los Primeros on the Epazote Real Trail
Taco Shop Poets, Logan & Sampson Street Longaniza Specialists
John & Shellita, Degrees of Nogales Soul Batter
Los Alacranes, Yaqui Tuners of the Vihuela Quesadillas
Víctor Carrillo & Marta López, Panitas del Moog Angelino
Lila Downs, Howl-Woman of the Mixteca Chocolates
Libertad Estrada, Conecta of the Electrosopes
raulrsalinas, Salmon Runner of the Libre Mantecas
Marissa "Volcanowoman" Riagoza, Comedianta of the Fresno Birrias
Bisbee & Southern Arizona Poets of Armadillo Delights
Lorna Dee Cervantes, Splasher of Mango Milagros
Junior Meléndez, Pilot of the Familia Tilichis

Vey & Yoli, Greggy & Bonni, Lizzie & Lolo, Louie Carlitos & Gloria,
Bobby & María, Seven Card No-Peekers of Saguaro Cariño
Tía Alvina Quintana, Founder of the First "Mexicatessen" in the Bay Area, RIP
Tía Teresa Rangel, First Chicana Swimmer at La Y en San Francisco
Austin Learning Academy, Mujeres con la Pluma de Chiltepe
Ramón García, Innkeeper of the Werewolf Cremas on 99
Centro Cultural de la Raza, San Diego, Survivors & Tolteca Cactus Whirlers
Jorge Robles, Harold Kirpatrick & Emilio, Tuners of the Soul Tree
Anthony Vigil, Obsidian Swirler of Moon Howl Jitomates
Andrés Montoya, Jim Sagel & José Antonio Burciaga, Sprinters of Soul Sabor,
RIP
G. Soto, V. Martínez, T. Álvarez & J. Herrera, Bards of Solar Ceviche
Gato Murguía, Marisol & Magaly, Innkeepers of Huehuetitlán Mondongos
F. X. Alarcón, Alfonzo Texidor, and Jorge Argueta, Compays de Ajito
& to all the poets casting their hearts into the sky
& all the trees in these pages & to the universe because she was first. ¡Om
y qué!

Self-portrait in a black mirror, 11th Street, San Diego, California, 1964

Notebooks of a Chile Verde Smuggler

Mamá's album page: Juanito in first grade; Mamá Lucha in photo booth, San Francisco, California, c. 1945; Border checkpoint detention shot of Abuelita Juanita (left), Tía Lela (top), and Mamá Lucha (bottom right), Juárez, Chihuahua, 1920s; and Great-Grandmother Vicentita Palomares (seated), 1890s

Abuelita Juanita and Great-Grandfather, Mexico City, c. 1889

Hard Curas on "C" Street

1436 "C" Street, late fifties,
San Diego, California

Show Mamá my right big toe infected and swollen. Ven aquí, she says.
OK, Mom. Just put your foot in this pan of hot water. Hold the toe up, Juan,
come on. OK, now, give me that razor. What razor?
Your papi's brand new Gillette. It's not brand new, Mamá.
'S OK, the hot water and the salt will burn the germs.

You ready, Juan?

Limpia for Walking into Clear Campos

Winter, Carbondale, Illinois,
late February, 1993

Step ahead, be careful—the ice,
you can slip.

Unloosen, breathe. Remember to breathe deep.
Unloosen. Swing to an easy beat.
Let your jacket become light, the sweet light
from the floating leaves of winter.
Sing to yourself. Follow the naked trees.
Sing

I drop my burdens
from my feet that guide them
I drop my burdens
from my ankles that turn them
I drop my burdens
from my calves that cup them
I drop my burdens
from my knees that rock them
I drop my burdens
from my thighs that run them
I drop my burdens
from my hips that churn them
I drop my burdens
from my sex that heats them
I drop my burdens
from my belly that smoothes them
I drop my burdens
from my ombligo that ties them

I drop my burdens
from the small of my back that cradles them
I drop my burdens
from my cintura that dances them
I drop my burdens
from my ribs that cage them
I drop my burdens
from my breasts that nourish them
I drop my burdens
from my mid-back that protects them
I drop my burdens
from my shoulder blades that build them
I drop my burdens
from my shoulders that salute them
I drop my burdens
from my upper arms that wrap them
I drop my burdens
from my elbows that swing them
I drop my burdens
from my forearms that caress them
I drop my burdens
from my wrists that pull them
I drop my burdens
from my hands that grasp them
I drop my burdens
from my fists that defend them
I drop my burdens
from my fingers that find them
I drop my burdens
from my neck that balances them
I drop my burdens
from my head that circles them
I drop my burdens
from my forehead that honors them
I drop my burdens
from my eyes that picture them

I drop my burdens
from my nose that breathes them
I drop my burdens
from my face that covers them
I drop my burdens
from my lips that invite them
I drop my burdens
from my mouth that savors them
I drop my burdens
from my voice that soothes them
I drop my burdens
from my throat that swallows them
I drop my burdens
from my heart that lives them
I drop my burdens
from my lungs that fill them
I drop my burdens
from my stomach that knots them
I drop my burdens
from this body that holds them.
I drop my burdens.
I drop my burdens.
As I walk, I drop my burdens.
As I walk, I melt with the snow.

Immigrant Fortune Teller Machine

Lissen,
Bobo Chango—yeah,

you, rope-a-dope blues lover,
writer with a jinx on your ass, time is up
on your side of the block, betta' be adding up
your karma tortillas jus about now, 'cuz,
all the chips you've been collecting be gone
to the wind, man, so
lemme set you straight
in a nice way, got it? So,

whaddya gotta do,
Chango, is—begin again,
toss out your old coins,
your mamá ashes, your papá whips,
yo' bad boy lover pill-poppin' games
an' mos of all your fast talkin' total whack
communicating genius girl self out the door!

Ahright, Sugar, yeah,
thass what I say,

step on
out now, naked,
everything showing, yo'
true self,

not that slime bug collection you've been
showing at the parlour, no no, noooo

you know whadday mean,
yeah, Chango, now,
iz up to you, you gotta trow out all that razz
matazz affabet', all them piles & stacks
of crosswords, those tiny pronunciation
dictionaries, the ol' memory power
tapes and that self-enlargement machine,
you know whad am sayon, OK?

Out wid it
out with all them hoodlum paintings of yoself,
out out, I said,

this is the lass stop before you
hit Phoenix, you know that next place you say
you are bound for, I see your ol' truck outside,

hissin', gettin' all shook under the sun,
outside, with that fine weasel sitting
on the red leather cushion next
to the wheel,

still rappin' about Desert Storm
comix & the great stash of bodies in the trunk
all the way from Tegucigalpa, yeah, yeah

I know, I heard it true
the grave vine, talking about the Virus in
air, grinning at you, adding up your DNA
like Fritos and bean dip, I can hear it from
here, yo' radio blastin' out,

yeah, about the Chain People,
the Chain Colonies, the hunger artists in search
of chicken sandwiches, the new bands of rape dogs,

it's my language anyway, sucker
so

whadelseiz new,
you going to ask me a new new
question today?

You come up with somethin'
new new? So tell me then, wha?
Did you say new, did you say Shakyamuni?
Did you say Shotinyotoey? In the hall,
the fast destiny velvet ball, is that what I hear

I heard you say
something? Or maybe you were jus laughing
in that fast high mariachi voice you got
from whoknowswhere, San Francisco? Yeah,

you jus bopped
in on the sneak,

but I'm tellin' you, don't
you come heah nomo
thinking I'm going to put up wid you &
your razz about yo'self and all those yellow
papers you carry in your fish bag,

yeah thass
what it smell like, fish, good ol' mackerel,
wrapped in newspaper, yeah, yeah, you call it
something else, you always call it something
else, you come out with all those fancy hooks,
those scratchy little phrases, those words, yeah
those hooks,

thass what you call them, wordyhooks,
and you spin around me like an Italian
Puerto Rican boxer with all the moves an'
handsome serious faces you make

saying
you look good in any hat south of Broadway,
but, I'm telling straight up sugar, time is up, see
that door to yo' left,
no that one, muchacho,
the one
to your left I said, yeah

the one cracked
dopen, the one with all those tiny smoky
black bluish candles popping inside, gold
smoke and shadows, red vases blurrin'
wavin' into watery insects on the wall there,
some kind of holiday, like,

come on now,
I told you all about that door
long time ago, remembrrr, yeah, you remembrrr,
that first almost infinite day
when you came
up to me by yo'self,

yo' mamá and papi
still alive then, I think they were havin'
coffee and apple pie a la mode over there
by the newsstand, and your father was talkin'
big 'bout buyin' some kinda land in Kingman, Arizona
paying thuddy dollars a month from the Welfare check
sayin' he was goin' to leave it you,
but he was jus
a li'l too old for those things, his light was

'bout gone by then, then, well you know the res.
Now sugar, one lass time,

you go now, get on
out now, leave those old cardboard boxes here,
ain't nothin' in them anyway, jus leave them
right heah, & go on out there, time is right,

I can tell by the way people are shuffling
their feet & the shadows 'cross the fences,
time is time, jus smell the wet night rollin' in,
you know how my green blue blouse
always gets a li'l tight jus about now,
rain comin' in, maybe,

my customers drop a coin,
ask me 'bout the yellow sparks of sirens, wild crows
flyin' up to the saints carved outside the cathedrals
askin' same ol' questions, perched on the glass
against this glass, jus like you

they shiver and whisper like in an ol'
movie house, 'bout to begin, I tell 'em
the nun & St. Peter jokes 'bout to spin out
to the asphalt one more time, yeah, yeah

I think the weasel is waiting for you,
leave me the rope, doncha worry
'bout a thing, jus smooth your way out
by yo'self, whistle up

with yo' tiny crooked musical faces
thass your existence, Bobo Chango boy,
thass it.

book two   Chile Con Karma

Tía Lela at twelve years of age, First Holy Communion, Mexico City, 12/8/1920

Óyeme, Mamita
STANDING ON 20TH & HARRISON

Tortilla Flats, where railroad tracks still cut across the street, Bekins storage warehouse and the old Regal Select brewery specters over me in reddish smoke rings, this bawdy corner where Tía Alvina ran her Mexicatessen, La Reina, packing tortas de jamón con queso for the truckers while Cousin Chente and me folded coquitos into sharp hot pink and white packs on a steaming iron griddle. Can still hear Cousin Tito in the back of the Victorian slap congas to a Cal Tjader groove at the Black Hawk. Tío Beto upstairs patient and quiet talks to a fifties thick mike in "El Hi-Fi" room, his makeshift studio, recording a Mexican oldies show for Radio KOFY. It's been a while since we've talked. Óyeme. Must be around half past ten. Time for a merienda with pan dulce, right?

Remember when you told me one night in the early eighties, "I am worried about you, Juanito?" And I turned around from my miniature writing table, second floor Capp Street, apartment #10 and froze? Your voice had a ruffled and serious timbre. Recognized it and looked away from the small amber light above my head. "I see you looking at yourself put letters on paper," you said. All my illusions of being a poet shrank, the wings of the eagle-writer that sees all twittered into the shadow of a sparrow, a wavy blot of cold ink on a yellow legal pad.

Undelivered Letters to Víctor

#1

Late November, 1996

You point your finger at me and say that if one Chicano or Latina makes it, then we all make it. The East Coast publishing centers will start dialing your number, you say. You mean a kind of literary intimacy, a Latina pulp osmosis? Is that it, Víctor? You gotta be right. Something's going on. You keep on telling me that Chicanos are authentic Americans, that this is the first lesson. This takes me back to Pocho-Che days in San Francisco when we hoisted up Che Guevara and Lolita Lebrón as our American figures. *América* we chanted through rain, meetings, snow, demonstrations, more meetings, cuffs, and sleet. We are the real thing, you tell me. Been breaking new ground for decades, inventing ourselves, a new set of categories, fresh art forms, an authentic discourse, we been hashing it out, without much to go on, except this fiery salsa fuel inside, we put up cultural centers on pennies, Teatro Chicano, Teatro Latino, lesbian ensembles, Latino gay performance, we did it with khakis and wino shoes, you name it, we've broken through the wall, against all odds, from frijoles to murales, from stealing sacks of chiles to reappropriating our language and sexualities. Now that's American, carnal, you tell me, with your raspy voice. American originals. Maybe this is the key—invention. Is it possible?

Original?

New York City Angelic

JOSH, MY SON, SAID
En Route to New York City

Josh, my son, said he'd probably show up with champagne and fire poems. "Fire writing," he said. Can't get over the simult-intensities between fathers and sons. My mother's intensity to me: mother son: my own father Felipe, his quiet fires / 11th Street w/ amputated leg. Blood splash on the floor razor cutting his toenails—ol' México style deep gash w/ diabetes. This is where he began to die in a mad push toward rebirth: Chihuahua corn farmer campesino orphan train jumper teen travel kid to El Norte Cheyenne, Wyoming & the myth continues in its Ptolemaic ellipse back and forth to me. In that creative last tiny torrent he began to build:

2×4's

hammers

& 7" nails he began to hammer. Builder campesino at the age of eighty-two. Shuffler with the right foot draggin', talker, open-cuento style, nonsmoker, Baptist Mexicano English-speaking coat & hat man, white shirt & long johns—he began to build. After his last visits to Tijuana whorehouses at the age of eighty-two. After his last son, Juan Felipe at the age of sixteen who wandered. I wondered in silent cathedrals packed in illusion-sins & books on Zarathustra & Schopenhauer & Nausea at Mission Beach San Diego on Saturday mornings, on the R bus to Belmont Park, after my inside world grew thick & golden & wet marooned & caught & knotted & lonesome urban in the street blind solar boy on his left wing. He began to build: orphan drinker of goat milk & woman honey, seeker in a worn brown suit, Denver, 1907, a few blocks from the railroad station: now, hitched with my mother, out of wedlock, illegal w/o papers—naturalized before the world in 1924, with large speckled friendly hands, seed planter, potato fryer, proverb speaker & cuentosayer & more cuentos about the "bald man, the itching

man, and the runny-nose man"—or when spit turns to ice in Denver. That
figure, that man on the down slope in San Diego, mid-sixties w/ the Beatles
on the tube, Ed Sullivan in bluish black & white on the 9" w/ one John
Coltrane "Settin' the Pace" album and one Dion album on my sofa—no
record player. He began to build, w/ Vietnam smoldering, w/ Mexico
expanding into Díaz-Ordaz grenadiers in Tlatelolco, expanding from the
Romantic moon swoon songs of Pedro Infante & his metal plated frontal
lobe, dead now, gone into another last plane crash, his mariachi suit moist
in semen, broken guitars & all the young sharp haired & hi-toned &
prayed-out Mexican boxers dancing in the Tijuana bullring—El Ratón
Macías vs. Davie Moore in the rain among thousands, in the mesh-light
culture carriage of Catholic devotions. My father w/ a busted vessel & torn
walker foot bleeding nonstop express to oblivion, destiny—Renada town;
he began to build a new leg, a 2×4 campesino leg. Make sure he can
continue the flight-spiritual, the flight to my mother w/ pains in the belly,
w/ blood alarmed in her menstruation womb. She caresses a cat over the
torn sarape sheet & she looks away as I take her photo gaping hole openness
of our tiny apartment, in that place San Diego, in the midst of things, the
world dividing, exploding, damaged, sewn back through stone, grass, rocks,
capillaries, desert & trains.

Do the meditation:

The father guitar cuento song eternal
The mother no longer sacrificial, yet holy
The son, now walking, always walking
The house, gone up in tribal ashes, gone
South to emptiness
Gone to the earth sky river melody
No chain
No shame
No name.

Greyhound Depot Chavalo, San Diego, '57

At the jukebox,
playing "One Night" by Elvis,
Greyhound Depot, San Diego, '57

Me & Gabby Arteaga and his brother Tony from Phoenix. Gabby has a moon face & Tony is pretty close to Woody Woodpecker. Gabby's father runs construction & the apartments where I live—1346 C Street. We roll downtown with my mom and dad, second street, into the depot. Bust into the lockers, suck up some duffel bags, cigarette lighters, hard shoes from the Army Surplus. Come back to the wood bench, chew on some Walnettos, crawl into the curled space, elbow each other and watch people sleeping or going somewhere. Gabby throws his arms over Tony's shoulders. I throw them over Tony & Tony over me.

Watering Cebolla While My Father Burns Leña
Escondido & Vista days, 1955

Step down from the traila early morning, 6 A.M.

My dad burns some leña. Hear it sighing, then it whistles with a sharp ache,
the wavy smoke rises from the yard. It tells me the day tastes good. My jefito
leans back on the box-trailer made with plaster, wood slabs & two axles
from an abandoned Ford, drinks una taza de café, looks out to the tiny lot,
where the corn we planted is up six feet. The quiet air is sweet. I take it with
me as I walk down to the cebollas. They're coming up good—shower them
carefully, cut the hose water with my fingers, high above the plants. The
water mixes with the tomatoes and creates another universe, a deeper green
blends into the earth when it's wet. Look back to the trailer. The milpa
sways, small offerings come to me, gentle winds.

New York City Angelic

LISTEN CLOSELY
Grupo Pedrada, wherever you are

Listen closely to the United pilot's statement about fixing
the luggage compartment before takeoff.
Examine your pasta with peaceful eye, then proceed.
The sun lanes coming down on the Castro are distributed equally
over the Mission District, as the clouds permit.
Choose garlic without thinking.
Pick up the phone as if you are washing your hands.
When the mayor speaks or let us say those in government, think
of pigeons in flight, think of pretzel snacks for them.
Take in the piece of sky over you at this moment.

The word *Halifax*
The word *orgasm*
The word *atom*
The word *inside*

See if you can spell them the same way.
Dig that tunnel a little faster.
Dig that tunnel a little gentler.
Remember Hans Castorp?
Remember Trotsky wrapping his small stout arms
around Frida's white hard torso?
Count (V. Martínez does this) the grass blades popping back up through stone
(the stone in front of your apartment).
When your leg goes slowly, massage is best.
Pat yourself in the kidney area and you'll do wonders.
A Harley isn't an extreme thought.
Lesbianism isn't an ism.

Think about the tidal wave in your dreams.
Draw the tidal wave in your dreams.
Write for children as often as possible.
Walk in nonpremeditated patterns.
Walk in meditation patterns.
Alfalfa is a good beginning.
If you must make a mirror, do it outside of prison.
Remember Hikmet.
Remember Rodnoti.
Remember your sixth-grade clown work—it will come in handy.
When your plane takes off, all you got is a tray table.

Eat Union strawberries.
Eat Union grapes.
Fondle your water.

If New York pizza happens, go with it.
Keep breathing, especially in times of stillness.
A donut has meaning.
Destroy meaning as often as you can.
A tattoo may suit your anger.
Write a letter to a dead one, they like to read things,
the nights are quite busy, though.
Instruments made out of soap feel better.
Lentil soup is the food of saints and hookers.
When the plane takes off, lean back, don't fight it.
If you stare at a cloud at eye-level, know that it can kick your ass.
Burritos & lox can work.
Bananas & cream can take you where you want to go.
Noodles & fried sardines can work.
Do the Hully Gully as a fiscal report.
Grade papers with cilantro.
The sole of your feet is the soul of your mind.
At Washington Square park, a Chicano poet is munching
on a mortadella copa salami gorgonzola smeared sandwich
thinking about nothing.

At Dolores Park by the Church Street train tracks, there is a kid
placing stones on the rails, a wino sings.
At Aquatic Park, Jimmy Biala plays tumbao for Alcatraz, just in case.
The muni pier is a J for the bird rolling down from the sky.
If I had a hammer, I would paint it red.
Chinese red in the year of the ox is good.
Mexican black brings happiness.
Ceramic bowls hold your reflections with tenderness.
A wooden spoon speaks louder than a metal fork.
Gracias. Gracias. Gracias.

Don't Worry, Baby

This one's for you, Lenny

I worry about comedians who call me to back up their old Communisms

I worry about teen Chicanas advertising Jehovah at the bakery

I worry about exotic birds learning too much English

I worry about Sub-Comandante Marcos getting acne under the ski mask

I worry about feminists who want to identify Cubans in the room

I worry about tourists who think maids are natural

I worry about the governor's face muscles

I worry about disc jockeys who feel "enemy music" is a genre

I worry about the Dalai Lama strolling into a Sicilian seafood restaurant

I worry about writing workshops using hacksaws

I worry about Bill Cosby's karma

I worry about the return of folk singers

I worry about people who use the word *folk*

I worry about OJ's parenting methods

I worry about E. coli in Congress

I worry about Spielberg's next ethnic movie

I worry about New Age music repeating itself

I worry about drive-bys low on gas

I worry about the high cholesterol levels of Mariachis

I worry about soybeans invading Chicago

I worry about congeros who use Vaseline

I worry about little boys who memorize surgical procedures

I worry about Black and White panels

I worry about the flakes in breakfast cereals

I worry about what an elevator does to men

I worry about the receding hairline of trees

I worry about the innate anger of clouds

I worry about Zen priests dolled up in Hugo Boss suits

I worry about jazz running out of improvisations

I worry about Beijing doing Elvis

I worry about Russian women becoming rednecks

I worry about ethnics who claim four races

I worry about computers with bomb icons

I worry about artists who emphasize the word *visual*

I worry about Mexicans digging their stereotypes

I worry about X-mas sales in May

I worry about poets who believe in publishing

I worry about the word *alien* becoming too familiar

I worry about churches looking sharper than Macy's

I worry about the ass on the other side of the glass ceiling

I worry about the day having hours, minutes, and seconds

I worry about children with careers

I worry about conversations turning into exhibits

I worry about the continuous supply of tomatoes

I worry about fast foods in prison

I worry about impatient stop signs

I worry about brain shaving

I worry about battery-operated suicide machines

I worry about couples who date

I worry about Stephen King's supply of vitamin D

I worry about the next German lesson

I worry about cigars rolled in Maine

I worry about trendy transfusions

I worry about Oprah's penchant for T-shirt bed sheets

I worry about performance art going into the poultry business

I worry about kindergarten teachers whose clothes match

I worry about copy-cat do-gooders

I worry about the DNA chain getting loose

I worry about husbands on the phone

I worry about glossy 8×10 murder snapshots

I worry about nurses with no pay hikes

I worry about the dishwasher's revenge

I worry about assembly plants making plans

I worry about a faster way to process fries

I worry about tacos, pizzas, ribs, and bagels running out of steam

I worry about old fogies who stand up for the King of Beers

I worry about insurance agents posing as poets

I worry about a soprano sax replacing the mood of pain

I worry about smog in my retina

I worry about the complexion of beans

I worry about forces that get armed

I worry about the Mexican baker's death wish

I worry about oyster bars going straight

I worry about pro-life men with bulging bibles

I worry about blues without color

I worry about sex without sardines and cream soda

I worry about cut flowers on dirty graves

I worry about nuns with extra-large shoes

I worry about the seriousness of high-grade mascara

I worry about the Gauguin poster in the coroner's office

I worry about recruiters searching for color

I worry about carbohydrate lobotomies

I worry about rock cocaine as a vocational mining industry

I worry about smiling obituaries

I worry about the interpretation of death-row graffiti

I worry about the liverwurst in Bangkok

I worry about monolingual emergency signs

I worry about friendly status countries

I worry about the word *poet* being replaced by the word *Narodnik*

I worry about VFW halls that have Taco Thursdays

I worry about dancing in front of meat-eating seagulls

I worry about walnuts that resemble human innards

I worry about guys locked up so they can write

I worry about Picasso Tupperware

I worry about the army's knowledge of mountains

I worry about cowboys in rocket ships

I worry about rappers entering a spelling bee

I worry about the dead never speaking up

I worry about chickens in robot suits

I worry about the third kiss

I worry about proms as delivery rooms

I worry about the drug traffic parked in the White House
I worry about high school cafeterias as artillery ranges
I worry about what I am saying
I worry about the word *Mexican* having an X
I worry about people who say "Don't worry, Baby."

June Journals 6-2-88

Thursday

Apparitions in flesh:

A sad-eyed blond woman drives a flashy red-orange Audi thru the chasm of a basement parking lot underneath the towers of San Jose's new and expanding middle-class utopia financed by the nameless. She presses the accelerator biting the meter ticket between her front teeth.

Two watermelon Latin Percussion congas

lean on a display case at the back of Gonzaga's Pawnshop on Market Street. I am on my way to the bank to repair a bounced check. I wonder if Gonzaga's daughter is at the back, in the barred credit room vestibule pushing the electric button to let another Joe through the shrunken door. I remember hocking my Les Paul electric guitar for $100. I felt like I was selling my soul to a guy who reminded me of Tin-Tan, the great Mexican comedian. I didn't know whether to laugh or stab the devil.

I wonder how much those congas are.

Óyeme, Mamita

WHAT IS THIS "LOOKING," THIS "SEEING" YOU MENTION?

Were you talking about my intentions, my self-made pulp office, a feeble cathedral of signs, or something more like a Dalí explosion of multiple perspectives colliding in their futile leaps toward a living presence or was it a time-animal? This rodent, deadened, this tiny brown life that doesn't speak because it cannot breathe, this puppet of forgotten and impossible cuneiform. I look at my self put letters on paper and all I can conjure is the loss of time, the delving into bodiless terms and the thousand layers of empty space around me. The ink is mind. The mind has no barriers. The paper is breath. The word is deep silence. Óyeme, Mamita. You want me to live? This is what you mean, right? To live, to truly live as a true person, a Hach Winik, as the Lacandon Maya say. Remember when I first went down to Chiapas in 1970 and you sent me a money order for thirty-five dollars to San Cristóbal de las Casas, addressed to Hotel Jardín. I was out of feria, was scamming traveler checks in Tuxtla. "A true person"—the words move like water. Tortilla Flats moves like fire. What about words on paper?

Undelivered Letters to Víctor
#8

What are we renewing?
From what to what?
How long-suffering is the transition?

The concept is provocative, Vic, archaic, the whole thing about rising
from the ashes, dressed in campesino shorts, working off a molcajete, the
good ol' Indio Chicano stone mortar and pestle, mixing diverse elements,
mashing them into pulp and juice, into a new blood force. Resurrections
without a body, or is the body the words, the dead poesy? Resurrections?
Have we been locked into a religious frame, a vicious and regressive
underlying morality play without knowing it, the grammar of the Second
Coming? And yet things and moments seem pliable, transformative, we
move out into the open mix of coffee houses, homeless tenements, beaten
down chartreuse movimiento rooms, past the old Victoria Restaurant,
Gómez-Peña's loft on César Chávez Boulevard with velvet O. J. Simpson
paintings on the walls, New Age gargoyle trilingual lowriders, swamp art
spaces, Kulingtan workshops & Pinay poetics, verse-riffs and performero
doo-wop, mercados featuring papaya and jitomate sales, gentrified Victorians
cutting through the old Irish, Mexicano, and Latino neighborhoods; things
appear new, our poesy missions appear refurbished, then the fog from the
Pacific rolls in again, homicide stats pile up on the curb, more death, then
light, rain, more rain.

Foodstuffs They Never Told Us About

Burnt tortillas
Gizzard pie
Serial killer pralines
1,000 reams 20-pound paper, white bond
Teriyaki ink
Bottled sweat
Levis wine
Hibiscus blintzes
Suicide under houseboat
Earthquake air
Cirrhosis bark
Thumbnail shrapnel
Chrome mayonnaise
Hijack tickets with free pastrami
Beige sofa mist
Midwest brick
Fleshy border crosses
Caramelized bone crucifix on front lawn
Pawnshop bread
Swiss bank borsht
Plutonium mustache oil
Baby Gila fangs in tights
Porno bird in sepia
Cuban correctness crepe
Ancestors in English mousse
Literary agent succotash
Presidential hotel waffle
Million Man neuralgia
Executive chicken
Lethal injection sugar

Penalty phase shoulder

Cloned pancreas

Marijuana grocery bag

Federal defense gingerbread man

Crack croissant

Cross-gender piroshki

Freud's cigar

Green cards in apologia sauce

Belgrade ethnic detergent

Sex worker adrenaline

Middle-class petit-bourgeoisie butcher paper

Donut with baton

Bertrand Russell's argument unwrapped

Nougat-center fondle

Mex yard-work knee salsa

Los Angeles with a side of destruction

Asbestos lobster

Cyber milk

Intestinal surveillance spaghetti

Sheep brothers

Administration flagellation suite

World Trade Center au gratin

Triple homicide rug malt

Unabomber sunrise

Royal Mercedes dipped in Prozac & whiskey

Yo' bones on the rocks

At the Mississipi Delta Blues Festival
Fast nights in Davenport, Iowa, 1989

In my house, camaradas. Even if I am 2,300 miles from the best taquerías in
Dinuba, Califas, or in Salinas at Olivia's. Front row, off the barbed wire
fence with los bikers. Okies & the hard leather women, long hair pulled
back like plastic, dream-eyed and reddish. Otis Clay on a Victorian stage, a
café con leche leisure suit, roaring thru the earth mud. Over Mississippi
black-juke water this floating Sonora rock desert, this blue chunk of
Yucatán. Above us, light poles & smoke blasts from the burnt boll weevils
loving the hot tungsten. La gente rubs against me. My shoulders are wet, in
tent steam, we rock the night prayer, our hands reach up, calabaza con
azúcar, cuero con almendras, yerbas locas, dark flesh in gri-gri velas, red
jackets blessed by the delta. Margarita's eyes are blurred halfway into the
ground, stones & tierra gone wild, opened up, I stand on the bench,
swinging my hips to the tragic bass & the sex water of the saxophone.

Patrick Henry Elementary, San Francisco, Sixth-Grade Class Photo

for the class of '61, room 102 &
George Ng, who taught me how to
crab-net &
count in Chinese

That's me in the middle row, looking goofy

with my Sears & Roebuck shirt. Yeah, I know Sears & Roebuck doesn't even exist anymore. Yeah. Next to Alfreydo Bautista—the carnal with a checkered shirt. Big Teresa to my left. I don't know why but she could be my sister. Then there's Moses, the Black vato sticking his neck out in the middle row. He's almost as tall as our teacher, Mr. Hayden, an ex-Sergeant from the army. Mr. Hayden lets Alfreydo & Gilbert, the Italian, duke it out in the cloakroom. After the math lesson, Mr. Hayden asks, "You guys finished?" We make up our own theater. Yolanda Palomares, the giant, is next to Big Moses. Please don't mess with Yolanda at recess, not even Moses does. Get your ass whipped good. On the other side of Mr. Hayden, big bad Rudy Quintoniles. The girls like him, especially Sylvia Trujillo, right under Yolanda the giant. Sylvia & Rudy ride on the bus next to each other. All of us take a bus to Patrick Henry every morning because our school, Marshall, only goes to fourth, this is sixth.

The problem with Rudy is his upper lip. You can see it's kind of wavy, doesn't know what to do. The wavy lip gave him away at the St. Charles bazaar where he tried to look mean by the "Spin the Wheel."

On the top row meet Nathan Botello, he's the only guy with that kind of name. You know anyone called Botello? Botello & me had it out at lunchtime. Smashed his mouth, chopped my knuckles. Both lost. Called my friend George Ng some nasty name. Something about being Chinese. Ng is right next to Botello. It's not his best shot. I think Ng's got a bronca. Maybe it's with Juan Escobar, wearing glasses and smacking his lips, or with Dennis, el mocoso, the kid at the end of the row. Checkered shirt too.

You are not going to believe this. The tough guys are the ones on the floor, tiny sitting boys. Darnel Hall, behind the board, a perfect smile, Hosea, next to him with his arm around "Chilito," again sporting a checkered shirt. At the other end, Bobby Guajardo with a butch wax conk and George Calandrias, with a conk & a twist. Calandrias & me got busted at Woolworths next to Leeds, before X-mas, stuffing our shirts with key chains. Years later, Guajardo got shot in the face. So did Hall. Don't know about the girls except for Ana de Rose, above Guajardo, Portuguese, who I crooned for under her Victorian flat on Van Ness Avenue or La Nancy, wearing bobby socks under wavy Rudy, headed for Everette Jr. High (by the way that's Dolores García, next to La Nancy, giving you that chinga look), to the right of Yolanda, the giant, Honolulu Angeles—in deep blues, with a pony tail, she was the one.

Machofilia(s)

Tobacco socks
Leather forks
Redwood boxers
Spit instead of tears
The obscure insides of a Swatch watch
Guinness Record tattoos
Cremation in a mug
Horse naming as an Olympic sport
Napalm impressionism
Christian Bullet associations
Hitler's jeans
Cement talc
Copper-plated Grand Canyon
Grinding as an art category
Dostoyevsky class rings
Valdez oil spill polyester print shirt
Toothpick wrenches
Viet Nam rope tricks
Airport sculpture
Valvoline deodorant
Siamese cats on glue
Date with bank teller machine
Arson black
Rabbit tea
Antelope on a key chain
Howard Hughes comb
Smart bomb in traditional red
Power suit Nagasaki
Pall bearer glove liner
Demolition derby fender prints

Stethoscope scars

The word *zygomatic*

Restraining odors

Forensic lunch bags

Still life with belly incision

Air Force recruiter office air freshener

Corporate handshake molds

Camouflage wedding ring

Salmon egg hand warmers

Bossa nova generic CD

Twenty-volume pictorial encyclopedia on Mars

Kuwait Campground Guide

Rib-eye face cream

Distance-o-matic Enhancer Machine

Millennium Omens

Van Gogh's self-portrait on Tylenol bottles
Gone with Hertzegovina novel
Electric shock leadership seminars
Grecian skin color shampoo
Burger mutation zoos
Fetal malts
English Only voluntary implants
United States of Bill Gates (USBG)
Toxic waste cults
Kindergarten taxidermy
The sale of California to the Munich Group
Ethnic identity as an official mental disorder
Mass grave workshops
Radiation albacore varnish
Macy's & Mussolini merger—Massy's
Child molestation fiber jumpsuit
Galactic Garbage Distribution Center
"Watusi Titanic" replaces Texas state name
The abolition of French bread
Spanish as the official correctional facility language
JanitorWorld opens at Disneyland
Virtual funerals
Tongue detectors
Armored truck neighbor tours
Sewer malls
Transdermal accent remover
Ocean glue music
Lightning museums
Russian wetbacks
Motorized torture button kit

Gas chamber board game
Grasshoppers for the blind
Air shows by the homeless
A numeral alphabet
Antloaf
Insecto hair growth enhancer
Organ transplant discount center
Suicide hammer sale
Voltage prophylactics
Neural tube piercing at birth
Cryogenic adultery
Diet blood
Davidian carrot cake bake sale
Silicon breast Boddhisattva

Undelivered Letters to Víctor
#30

Have you seen the young ones, the generations of Raza poets and writers spit out "Aztlán," talk about new stone idols, ring up workshop poetics, quote Archibald MacLeish, Marianne Moore, Berryman, then "Chicano power" and "Quetzalcoatl" one more time? And the gallon of hand-me-down nationalist sewage? The New gnaws at me. Or is it ground zero? Is it the fact that we never did fall, truly alone and shivering, into the furnace of an authentic experience and explosion of community across assigned boundaries and voices, into the colossal and marvelous thing called change, called reality, this Thing-just-like-this? Wipe my face, squint, make sure I say what I mean.

June Journals 6-1-88
San José, Califas
First Street Project Band days

As Chicano artists, we have always pulled out our images, landscapes and
symbols from the gut to the page, from the bile to the open forum; historias
terribles of our people, our time; historical suffering in vitro.

It is time to quench another thirst, perhaps, a greater thirst, one that is more
insatiable, delicious: pull out the monsters from the Colossal Inside, North
America; the gargoyles of power, our soft-spoken and concentric-eyed
representatives; much better than the familiar grimacing representations
of ourselves.

What have we learned from our Capitalism? The decapitation of our joys?
The desire for simulations of consciousness?

I love sculpture, the art of breaking space.
Writing, the quarry.

Óyeme, Mamita
LA REINA IS GONE. BEKINS IS OUT.

The brewery has been replaced by shrewd developers, a school, a condo, a
boy with a tattoo that reads Destroy. The Mission District is El Salvador in
Spandex and Nike grafting, Nicaragua in Reebok skins and a slip of
Guatemala in Zenith blue cathode light. The old Flats of the fifties and early
sixties have gone up in smoke. Electric worms pulse through the streets,
their one-eyed heads glow meth, heroin, and other bad stash. Drive-bys and
cappuccinos, ODs and mango sherbets, street rape and Hindu saris slit up to
the dark cinnamon brown thigh. Your old optometrist still hangs his sign
over the chicken roast shop on 24th. Tía Aurelia's apartment on top of
El Pollo Loco, on the corner of 17th and Mission is the gateway for hookers
that cross their Johns to a nearby hotel or shuffle fast to an empty lot with
fences wagging like tongues. Don't forget the squirrel-eyed entrepreneurs,
lined up with scrolls of architectural drawings for one more pizzeria, one
more Chinese-Thai-Mexican-Italian-Irish print shop that will put out a
Guinness Record yield of ceramic cups and neo-leather luggage, devil
decals for the youngsters, papaya powder, Bogart lapels. Oaxacan trinkets,
Frida Kahlo and Joe Montana muslin shirts and Marilyn Monroe wigs. The
fog rolls in and covers the letters, the fishnet bodies, the night soil man
sweeping the asphalt with hot acid and the cucaracha jacket teen girls
howling like Ginsberg, in maroon eyelash drag, slouching toward a
boisterous and tender infernodise. Óyeme, this is where we are supposed
to laugh and dance and write and taste the bitter-sweet existence of our
royal jelly hearts—Mamita, óyeme.

June Journals 6-3-88

Yesterday I picked up an issue of *La Regla Rota,* a tough Mex-punk magazine from Mexico City. Bobby P. brought it over last weekend. He travels south to buy posters and trinkets and makes a decent living at it. We used to drink the daylights out of ourselves at Antonio's Nuthouse in Palo Alto when we were going to Stanford. Anyway, I was reading *La Regla.* Luis Zapata, gay Mexican novelist has a column. This is the dude that came out with *El vampiro de la Colonia Roma* in the late seventies winning the Grijalbo Prize. As a matter of fact, Frank ZenthroAmerica and I were jaunting through Mexico City that year, 1978. I had been given an award to study and assist a Stanford anthropologist doing work in Cárdenas, Tabasco, that summer. I had been churning the gears surviving my first grad year in the anthro department and now I was on my way south. Frank happened to be teaching a summer language course in Cuernavaca, vacation city for any would-be middle-class sunbather. I made it to Veracruz, Veracruz, one of my favorite hangouts. You sweat away the Bay Area and other bits of madness in the system. A tickling sensation ruffles your guts. Everything is a hundred times brighter. The food, the night, the sharp cerulean blue hotel rooms, the colonial whiteness, the ocean, the terrible sandstorm on the beach, the old folks dancing mambo on the street at midnight. I was at the depot ready to take bus to Tabasco. But, I decided to catch a flick, miss my ride, see a bit of Cantinflas, and think about my real next move. I dropped the project and split to Cuernavaca, met Frank and disappeared for a while. Later, back in D.F., we ended up cooling out with Gustavo, el Caballero, head honcho of one of the literary cliks of D.F. We ate at his fine pad on Nápoles. His maid made burritas. Burritas white flour tortillas stuffed with ham and cheese. A writer with a maid that makes burritas?

In Case You're Still Wondering about Racism

Consider the whip marks on your television set
Consider the clown voice you make at socials
Consider your summer vacations in Watts
Consider how you pronounce chile relleno
Consider your new Afro-Haitian collection
Consider the weave pattern next to your diploma
Consider how you fold your hands in J-town
Consider diabetes as a credit card
Consider your little black book
Consider Mao as your father
Consider Toña la Negra as your mother
Consider your daughter's use of bananas
Consider rice as the key subject
Consider the hips when you do your math
Consider the angel with a blonde fondue in your bed
Consider your upper lip while referring to Alabama
Consider your tidal wave dream
Consider the origins of your Zenith
Consider the weasel-like valet in the mirror
Consider 97% of modern art
Consider your Hawaiian tastes
Consider your singles overseas mail order catalogue
Consider mango truckers
Consider McDonalds on San Juan de Letrán Avenue
Consider the latest reverse discrimination scholarship
Consider the underground landscapes of your TV cable
Consider an Indian with Coca-Cola vertebrae
Consider the snarl on your slumming jacket
Consider the obscure beeps of negritude across your lawn
Consider the gardener's personal mileage chart

Consider your daily use of plastics

Consider a Western movie rerun

Consider the body sweat inside a Chevy trunk

Consider the iambic graffiti in middle-school cloak rooms

Consider getting stoned on potato pancakes

Consider the wrought-iron gate entrance to your crib

Consider outer space as your next adventure

Consider the stock phrase "we are all human beings"

Consider the Spanish-like pronunciation of your automobile

Events & Found Objects after the Blast

Ivana Trump's wedding band
Last presidential advisor stuffing raw oatmeal into a briefcase
Concentration camps on Broadway
Manhattan smashing into Burma
Kurdish looters roaming Coney Island
A camel on fire
Miami Dolphin touchdown with pizza crusts
Cicadas and cockroaches with berets
Hokkaido ice avalanche over Abilene
Charlie Parker coffee cup
Rice paper tents over the Golden Gate
Black tenor on Powell Street
Polo in San Quentin
Dogs on vodka
Girlfriend armored tank
Two livers in love
Embryos racing after an Elvis stamp
Bone soap
Blue Styrofoam corn
Gasoline Parfum
Club Monaco butcher knife
Eddie Palmieri island shirt
Hookers driving Greyhounds
Airport mice on expensive chocolate
Graceland drifts near Luzon
Worm language stop sign
Air Jordan shelters
Heisman bronze molars
Peccary with the Pope's cone hat
Los Angeles rubbing against Cabo San Lucas

Mars meteor flea market

Las Vegas burns in Oahu

Organ transplant fish bait on a hook

Redwoods rolling over Universal Studios

Shoe salami sandwich

A grizzly making porno faces on Wall Street

White Owl cigar

Goat buttocks on ice

Raft with three Microsoft millionaires sucking olives

Fidel Castro in bikini strolls through Miami ashes

Apache raid in Mexico City

Gortari confesses on Guadalajara Island

Havarti cheese lines

Two Fresno grape growers selling chupacabras T-shirts

Greenland remains intact

Madrid in Jamaica

Dalí's chartreuse reincarnation in the White House

Brazil in the shape of Santana's guitar

June Journals 6-27-88

A writer must deal with big questions, big deepness, big heart, big fist.

Big mind. How do we do it?

You know there are too many people pushing book covers, taunting their groupies with their radish-colored avant-nose. Too many military clowns standing at attention, guarding their field rat compound of style or anti-style or clique or anti-click. Too many traffic safety boys with a sour badge pinned on their trousers making sure the commuter horde stays in the proper parking lot poetik. San Francisco is Grid City. If you are a writer you belong to the Grid Generation. North of Market, the Post-Beat Pantheon and its sundry shadows. But, who speaks of South of Market, the Mission, the Castro, or West of Van Ness, the Haight, the Filmore? Who writes about a collective thrust of writers burning the old thrones: craft, male-centered institutions, heterosexual dominance, middle-class marathons, performance-focused relationships with the audience, muted apolitical consciousness, antisensual worlds?

Shall we huddle and smoke and shake hands and grin and then publish some sweaty-assed two-bit newsletter on this? Is this the extent of our voice in 1988? In June?

June Journals 6-29-88

I am looking at a tree and the TV wires above. My backyard hummingbird walks the rope. Stands. Listens. Observes. Flies in a perfect ellipse and warns others with a defiant click sound when it senses danger.

How do we get to the big questions? Real beginnings?

When I left S. Z.'s office I smelled an old sweetness. Charred wood, singed paint. The Vietnamese furniture store on the corner burned down last night. In '63 our casa burned down. We were living at 901 Tenth Street downtown San Diego, a few blocks from the public library and right across from Salazar's, a Mexican food joint. Those were the days when I would hang out in a used magazine store a block down on Broadway and check out *Life, Cosmopolitan, Photoplay,* science fiction, nude fotos, books on how to be funny. Shafts of light, here and there, musty—a giant caterpillar stomach, eating leaves from a funny paper garden somewhere above us all. Or I would bop to the waterfront all the way down Broadway slowing by the tattoo parlors and the refrigerator-sized jewelry stores. Elgins, Hamiltons, Bulovas and Chinese dragons and Okinawa black jersey jackets. And fire.

June Journals 6-7-88

Been thinking about Buffalo, an inmate at Soledad Prison where I teach a poetry workshop. He reminds me of Jamulie, a friend who spends time in L.A. truckin' hot chile peppers across Mexico for his dad's business. Buffalo smiles if you smile genuinely. He got thirty-two years for a mystery crime. I can't imagine what can get you thirty-two. Thirty-two to go. It could be a bit of a problem, but why not trade places? You and me. Twenty-four hours. Whaddya say? Jamulie would say something like that. I thought about it. It could be a gas. It could be a nightmare. Most likely a nightmare. For me, of course. On the other hand Buffalo strolls in and says hey baby, how ya' doin' kisses my wife and suddenly snarls at Marlene, my stepdaughter, who can't get off of a long reel of TV soaps and telephone marathons. Trade places? Trade places with a city supervisor?

Óyeme, Mamita

TORTILLA FLATS IS THE PLACE TO BE

There is hope. Yes, no?

Óyeme. It isn't that sugary "Hispanic" minority on the rise to the new world order kind of esperanza but something more like a Jackson Pollack frenzy-hope, dotted and jagged and splashy and messy, some fresh stinging fragrant high that jumps out of the wood, cement, the double earrings and lip piercings, the gelled hard and buzzed hair, the flying vapor from crazy Mexican panaderías on Hampshire and 24th, the Vietnamese—little Saigon cafeterias with their double doors open to the public, this is where I get to the ecstatic, the triple hit of cilantro with coconut milk and roasted kidney in chicken broth, the squid empanadas and the thick Samoan teen vatos shopping for Energizer batteries wearing towels wrapped like flowery skirts—the new energy is in here, with its wet nose working out the perfume, the new thing we are, the place we be at, the making of the world in the I's, the ahorita, now. You know, Mamita, óyeme. Tortilla Flats rolls in high like a wave then it simmers and disappears. Alone on 20th Street with my hands talking empty.

Man Goes Woman

When he orders a falafel and calls it a Phil
When he comes home and cleans his lips
When he refers to his socks during an interview
When he rubs his cheekbones in front of others
When he stops playing congas on his dashboard
When he uses his eyes more than his nose
When he shakes his thoracic area
When he attracts people in the office
When other men run into him by mistake
When he admires the tiny hands of infants
When women relax as he walks in through the door
When he acquires a distaste for history
When he would rather touch the top layer of a wave
When he listens to pauses
When guilt becomes his favorite topic
When he abandons barbecue pits and no one cares
When he smashes his computer over his father's portrait
When he realizes being alone is an art
When he can identify footsteps by gender
When the words he uses actually are connected to him
When he laughs like his grandmother
When he prefers to stay home and make plans
When he writes like a hurricane
When he burns his hands while others watch TV
When he can decipher measles a week in advance
When the pain below his belly is prophetic
When he organizes himself without anyone noticing
When his bible loses its military purposes
When he calls a sunset a sunset
When his Texas becomes smaller than her Idaho

When his belt is an ornament
When he pliés with a novel
When he talks before he eats
When his daughter listens to him
When terror and ecstasy are the same thing
When his promotion gets too private before it goes public
When his EKG chart is his only evidence
When his money turns to salt
When his Saturday night special wants to go out every night
When his bruises are just bad makeup
When he comes home & kisses the one he loves.

Abuelita Sofi Smokes Up la Cocina

Making 300 buñuelos
for las Hermanas at San Javier,
El Paso, Texas

La reina del aire,
that's what they call me, she tells me, porque sé caminar—talking about las
comadres at church. Yo me voy caminando, yo camino, she says again. She
laughs a little to herself, twists a bolt off the table leg with pliers. Abuelita
Sofi walks the miles across Huerta to Delta, past McClarity Elementary,
down Delta to San Javier, steps through the heat of El Paso, passes through
her lives from Segundo Barrio, in adobe alone with four children, to this
winding, downward wood road, she listens to the ragged winds, voices
again from Mt. Franklin where the rich live. Go with her to Food City, buy
chuletas, masa, and azúcar. Wait for her, as she talks it up with the manager,
el joven. Today, just 300 she says, maybe 330. La reina del aire, ja, las otras
en el sofá—yo no, yo me sé mover.

Óyeme, Mamita

ANOTHER CROSSING

This is what I am sensing. Tortilla Flats is the barometer, the long wooden spoon in the manteca. A different moment awakens the century. An exotic spirit drops its handkerchief and waits for us to pick it up.

Óyeme, Mamita, you always read. Newspaper columns, *Readers Digest, Look Magazine, Life, Photoplay,* and *La Opinión,* which my uncle Fernando insisted was the only paper worthy of a reading public, next to *El Esto,* which features soccer and boxing, the necessary Mexican mythology of Men in power for men in powerless positions scattered through Tortilla Flats, the Mission, and on all the way to Mexico City and its surrounding satellite villages and towns, like Tlanepantla, Chalmita, and Atizapán de Zaragoza where Tío Fernando was born. Atizapán de Zaragoza is now called Ciudad López Mateos after the Mexican president of the sixties, also a native from that town. All I can recall of Atizapán is the acrid and sweet smell of pulque taken from the hearts of full-grown maguey plants and my initials I carved into the cactus while I strolled around with Amelia, a teen girl from the village back in '61. Óyeme, Mamita, we were in DF, remember?. You cried in Xochimilco while the cameraman in another chinampa took our foto. Tía Aurelia was as usual scolding and heavy voiced, pushing you into a small bundle of remorse at the edge of the waters. I cried too. Mexico did not fit us then. We were going astray into another world. We carried the pain of so many border crossings and infernos. Mexico, Texas, California, the fields, the barrios, trailers, and welfare offices and curanderas with nurse implements attempting to cure you—and me. Óyeme, Mamita, maybe it wasn't a real illness you suffered, maybe it was how you carried all of us. My father Felipe who always moved and left us to see his other familia; my aunt Aurelia, my tío Fernando who insisted that I wear double-breasted suits and his thrift store bought men's shoes because he could sell them to you at a cheaper price; my uncle Beto and his large family, his radio show of the Golden Age of México, his advice as an older brother, his own entrapment in words, radio words, children and wife words, house words, American and Mexican words, something deeper too, Mamita, you, yes, you—your words, what happened to them?

Your words. It wasn't me, was it? It wasn't me you were talking about that night on Capp Street. It wasn't my abandon to a pile of yellowish scrabbled sheets. It was you, óyeme, it was you, Mamita—where were your words? Your scraps of little phrases gleaned from newspapers and books and missals, the ones you memorized and recited every day, the dichos, the leyendas, the adivinanzas, the corridos, those words, the prayers, the alabanzas, the stories, oh yes, the stories about coming from El Paso, coming from la Colonia de El Niño Perdido in Mexico City, about walking all the way to Lecumberri Prison from El Niño Perdido, about begging for food, about washing clothes, waxing floors, and cooking for the rich on Mt. Franklin in El Paso. You are the paper, óyeme, Mamita, you are the words, you. Not me. Look at yourself put words on paper—You.

New York City Angelic

I SIT AT GATE #9

I sit at gate #9 Fresno Wednesday A.M. Mechanics "fix" the late engines of
United en route on a sunny hot tense day—to SFO. I am worried about my
luggage—one piece with underwear and ironed blue shirt & pants for the
big fandango in NYC. Jet burns overhead as a Hindu woman in pink-milk
patch sari sits in front of me with her face up through the skylights & a
flowery ribbon on her hair, she looks up to the sky region—the jet—boom
blows & tears another pattern through the dome.

New York City Angelic

I WAS DOING A POETRY READING THING

I was doing a poetry reading thing, a tour with Amiri Baraka. We kicked it off at St. Mark's. Read "Señorita Black Velvet Latina" & did my usual pyrotechnics—which of course can kill you in a flash. The stuff's gotta be honest. Your face gotta be honest. Regardless. So, I looked into the crowd: well-kept, steely gray-eyed Americanos, all white, wearing the typical boxed and tight leather jackets & top coats (May), a herringbone here and there, mellow and febrile & organized & burnin' dendrites, eagles in Florsheims. Last time, yeah. Stayed in the same joint I'll be at tonight & tomorrow night—the Washington Square Hotel. Great façade, tiny busted rooms. I had to walk sideways through the semi-demolished halls. But, the entrance—gold mirrors, plants from Tahiti, bellhops like Robert Goulet or a similar look-alike. I was on a typical poetry-biz assignment. Called Jane Z., agent, & said that archetypical line, "Hey, Jane, I'm in town reading tonight at St. Mark's"—that's as far as I got. Next. Called Max K., publisher in the Soho. Said cool, walked a few blocks to his ninth-floor book office-warehouse with an aged secretary & went out to lunch. Salmon on a kaiser. In one of those mid-level lunch joints, a good place to chat fast, do the run down you're a fine writer & I know about ethnic jive lit good luck, enjoy your free olives. I couldn't believe the guy on the ninth floor in New York City knew more than me & about the Chicano Latino insider-trading biz— the who's hot, who's dead, who's being executed at this very minute in the pressroom ticker-tape machine. Walked out, burned. Suck in the trapezoids, the charred backs, the faces, huddled, fast corners, the guy on roller blades w/ bread rolls & flowers.

Things Religion Makes Me Do

Get horny with the wrong images
Pull weeds with my tongue out
Revive Lenny Bruce
Carve lotto numbers on soap
Suck apricot wine off shiny surfaces
Shave without blades
Sprinkle tartar sauce on my right pant leg
Cruise Polk Street with a can of water
Inhale under pressure
Long for mummy-shaped Italian pastries
Mix up Robert De Niro with my gangster brother
Use cellophane gloves while eating shrimp enchiladas
Argue about salt
Fear roses
Chain myself to fashion malls
Separate roast beef advertisements from the language
Revive Lenny for the second time
Shred anything with the color red
Paint camouflage spots on truffles
Chop off bedposts on Saturdays
Volunteer at police bake sales
Use more vowels than consonants
Consider a falling leaf as an abortion
Call a cloud a wimp
Work on projecting higher shadows
Surrender only my dull knives
Climb stairs with expectations
Bury money
Neglect my teeth
Harass lingerie workers

Use talc instead of tortillas
Slice bread once a day
Ignite toothpicks
Marry every fifteen minutes
Drink soda while ignoring my tongue action
Rehearse handshakes under water
Make reservations in parking lots
Scramble my face as a sign of intimacy
Point every ten minutes
Check the spelling of the word pigeon
Poke holes in kaiser rolls and search for vapor
Wear corduroy undergarments
Read with my head bowed down
Blink in front of dressing room mirrors
Never look at her lips
Talk to wood miniatures
Use barbed wire instead of Scotch tape
Never look inside her ear
Mispronounce the word Chinese
Handcuff small rodents
Write Charlton Heston sonnets
Sweep water
Act like I am listening
Execute foreigner plants
Observe silence
Keep scabs bleeding
Wait for people who never show up
Wear 100% wool Pendletons inside out
Excavate cherry-filled donuts
Sit back, cross my legs, and cry.

June Journals 6-23-88

I am turning right at Santa Clara Blvd at 10th Street. My lawyer, S. Z.,
a gentle older wizard who likes the San Francisco Mime Troupe told me to
cool it before thinking of buying a house in Iowa. I've been playing at
buying a house. Got no money. I told him Margarita and I were thinking
of opening an enchi-taco paradise parlor there. He believed me. Margarita's
Enchi-Taco Paradise. Imagine?

New York City Angelic
I HAVE AN APPOINTMENT

I have an appointment
at Ananda Books at 2:00. It's 1:10 & I may not make it. So, maybe next time.
I want to talk about po-biz, poems, collected etceterrah! I want to walk
smoothly, for the moment—in the rain. I want to remember the tender
open eyes of the children. How they got a kick when I said "the rain tickles
the trees." How the doves were coming to answer their dove calls but turned
back because their heads got wet. My head is wet. Everyone is talking about
growing the brain by the age of 1: grow the brain! I suppose the brain is the
ultimate sale, product, frontier, capsule, coin, cow, chicken, river, horse,
train, rubber, wheel, map, slope, over yonder there is a brain to plow, to sell
& sew, carry to market! Who owns the market? That is the old .75 question.
Bag it, baby.

New York City Angelic
BACK ON SCHEDULE
April 21, 1997

Back on schedule. Eatin' beans & receivin' e-mail. Makin' love & teachin' class. Binary option & terciary paths. Zooming at Hale-Bob comet & wondering about my life at the energy rim, serpentine endless knot of migrations, lives & transfigurations. The sky is clear. The signs of Big Change (it always looks like Big Change to me) come up, reveal themselves & I go dreaming. I go walking. Just got back from New York City. Seeing Johnny Marrón w/ beret & a kiss in the lobby of the Washington Square Hotel. Hung out with him & the Ezra Jack Keats camaradas and I noticed that Jews & Mexbloods have a lot in common, a deep looking. And I met up with Bee C., editor, good human being, sturdy woman & stayed at her house, "The Fleishman Estate," "a garage," she said. We laughed, talked books, ten ideas. Projects, she's game. I'm game. John M. put the stopper on me: Forgiveness, surrender & consolation. This is your homework, he said. Truth. I am on it. To forgive, to surrender, to console—John says. Maybe it's about forgiving myself, surrendering to myself, consoling myself. Things are up. I don't know what it is. I am sitting here by a round table, fourth floor, California State University, Fresno. Library. & I am taking time out. Punchin', writin'. Lay it out. Flow it out. Say it baby, say it. Baby, say it!

Talked to Heather, editor in New York who says she's leavin' the business. To write a novel. Talked about agents. An adult collection, offers (J.T.W from Boston wrote me about agent/author sign-up). Heather says she'll get back to me in a coupla weeks. This is good. Johnny Small Fry moves on to the Center Grill.

Cuñada Yoli, en el Jale

Rialto, California, where the sun wakes
before the gallos

I used to be a Superwoman.—Gloria Velázquez

Her real name is Frances, I call her Yoli, Margarita calls her Yolanda.
Accounting's her jale, in a desert town, grey-blue, making numbers meet
budgets. Last summer, Yoli was working for a car dealer near Federated,
where her thin son, Junior, packaged videos. I spotted a top-o-the-line
Camaro, steel smoke, encabronado, con mags y todo, at the front studio
window. Yoli, I said, maybe you can talk to the manager, tell him I'm
famous or something, get me a suave deal on the ranfla. She looked up,
reflective, from the ledgers, Estás soñando, cuñao. She set me straight. Later
at her house on Melrose after dinner, I noticed how she gazed over the sink
into the yard, I didn't know if she was watching for Tex, the mixed dog, to
eat the laundry or if she was going higher up, over the houses, the moving
sky, torn clouds going west away from all the chavitos with peanut butter
on their faces, far from the clap of dust, trastes, pink erasers, a kitchen table,
beaten with hours, with pencils.

Margarita Walks the Fields in Fresno

Margarita, stays in Fresno. I am out in Carbondale, writing, listening to snow drift into the ground. She writes and teaches too. We form mirrors with our lives. Hers reaches inside, into the moon she says, into her friends. She walks with her compañera, Anita. Anita Kozo who was a drum major in Fresno High, a Stanford Ph.D. in psychology. Anita says things like Whatever you are feeling is what you should be feeling, or, if you get stingy with yourself she calls you on it and tells you—you are a "withholder, ése." Margarita is small, her hands are made of milk, she has the aroma of thick leaves, eucalyptus & roses. Her hair flies in the wind, reminds you she has secrets. She makes circles on a small plate of sand and prays for the lost ones and for the new ones with tiny arms and for her students who rush through halls and for young women who are beginning. She prays with plants and stars right in front of you, her face goes around yours before you know it. We build a blue fire for our children, the ones far away and the ones that sleep in the same room with us. Relax your shoulders, she says. Relax your hands, your eyes, your back, and your legs—she smoothes me. Her voice covers me with important places, wet grass oceans, ice plant, red coral water, then oregano and romerito, then sage and yerba buena, then cumbias and guayaba. We speak in soft ways to know there is love between us. Margarita Luna I call her. She walks in a circle, with her friends, I know or alone as I am, sometimes, when we walk through ourselves, when we are apart.

Huerta Street Telenovelas
Sabor in the sun, El Paso, Texas

Where my suegro Beto le está mochando la nuka al cókono for the weekend
(he doesn't work at el Safeway anymore) & suegra Dolores le tuerce el
pescuezo a la gallina (she let's the gallina fly just un poquito, todo tilinki)
for the mole más tarde. La comadre Olivia López está cazando unos nopales
con guantes rayados de Circle K. Don Victoriano escarba next to the yerba
buena, wipes his face with an old pañuelo Pa' los ejotes, he says while
cuñao Jorge, el güerito, carries un bloque de hielo for the icebox & la
Marlene anda besukiando con el boyfriend. Y el Louie? My suegro asks.
Pos anda fuera, I say from the sombrita next to the Coleman cooler, todo
triliado, cuz he just got a cheke from the divorcio.

June Journals 6-5-88

I was invited to give a commencement rap a few weeks ago for the English Department at San Jose State University. A woman asked me what writers influenced me, who did I read? I said, my mother. Lucha Quintana. Have you heard of that writer? The woman's neck twisted. No, she wanted to know "what writers"! She wanted to ask the usual worn phrase. Ginsberg, Artaud, Nervo, Lorca, Neruda, Popa, Hikmet, Rodnati, Walker. These are the shadows—I should have told her.

My mother published a thousand poems and a thousand songs in the quiet air of our house. Recitals were held at any given moment, unexpectedly, during a pause in a dry conversation, or just during the day. Ask my soul-partner Margarita Luna Robles.

Tío Fernando & the Chamuco of Atizapán de Zaragoza
for the 17th & Mission Street years. RIP.

Eighty years plus now, lives in apartment #10, four TVs, seven radios,
fourteen wristwatches—same room for the last fifteen years. When my aunt
Lela died a year and a half ago, he said he'd go back to La Capital, move into
a house w/ wrought-iron windows. He's been paying on it for twenty-three
years. I'm staying here, he tells me. Voy a colectar my Sosho Sekurity. Going
become American citizen. Mi hermano Cruz can take care of la casa, I can
always visit him, he says. It's by the airport. Leans back in the cramped E-Z
chair, shivers. I ripped out el heatah. Nomás me pongo más sacos, that's
how he puts it. Tell me the cuento about the night of the chamuco, Tío,
I say to him. Puts on his green eyeglasses, his hands crooked from laundry
work. Well, ya te la dije, muchacho, pero OK, one night

—it's true
very late at night, I was walking
back to my padre's house
in Atizapán, a few miles from
La Capital. In those days
era puro campo libre. Maguey,
ríos, files. It was very dark
when I heard a ruido.
Every time I took a step,
it took a step. Every time
I walked faster, it moved
quickly behind me. Right
behind me. Didn't want to turn
back, no way. Got so bad
that when I got close
to a tiendita with a light on
I was frozen, el chamuco

was right behind my shoes,
no quería voltear. Yelled
out to Don Chon en la tienda
Por favor, Don Chon, who's
behind me? Please tell me.
I took a step and the chamuco
was still there, even with the
viejito watching me. I could
hear a strange brushing
sound, like fire, light
and sharp sounds, very light
lika a sombra, un espíritu.
Please señor, dígame, tell me
por favor. I was frozen now.
It was very late, couldn't
move anymore. La noche was
all around me, except
for the tiny light de la
tiendita.

Mira, chamaco, said
the viejito,
es una bola
de paja stuck to your zapatos.

Subtleties

Guys with clip-on ties that want to pin you down
Women with big dark eyes that detect lies sitting on your mustache
A lover with one easy killer move
Fast-talking Post-Mod Existentialists that mean nothing
Loud poets with tiny words
An explosion of Puerto Rican merengue while choosing apples
Business letters that smell like pomegranate
A religious fanatic with the face of María Félix
Chiapas while doing the laundry
Lox in a state prison wood shop
Aztec sushi
Bomb smoke in the shape of a derby hat of the thirties
Cortázar novel next to him naked
Wrapped cream cheese at the murder scene
Tiny words that spell out your future
The obsidian beauty of an insect in heat
Love smoke
The semblance of Hoffa mixed into a Vermeer
Silent pipes
A cherry red Gretch electric guitar in bed
Queen of England bowing with a tincture of self hate
A tabloid mogul uttering the term *compassion*
Childlike carved flowers in the jury room wall
Zen toilet without a hole or a seat
Carnations instead of steak
Republicans with forced Iroquois accents
Group hate perfumes by color
Islam in the trees
PCP bullets
A lie in the algebra

Devonian landscapes on her lips

Flush sound silencers

A Flamenco fist

Peruvian shaman stir frying pasta

The retributions of a redwood

A zebra mirror

Satie inside the crashing glass

Car salesperson buttock acid print

Nervous dimple that wants to disappear

Shy neon

Soldiers taking time out to scoop the red grease

Face job entropy

A $twenty at the foot of the Buddha

The art of churning dirty needles in holy water

Ten tons of mutant hormones hanging over the state capitol

Offering range chicken on the side

The silent big bang of the universe

The Y in Hollywood

Guatemalan Mayan corn seed sprouting sideways toward Helsinki

Mammalian apologies

A Picasso fixing itself every time you check it

Premeditated homicide conferences in the administration building

Woman at the bank with violin case.

Fuzzy Equations

Humility + oppression + a Virgin – territory = Latin America

Democracy + annihilation by color × 12 = Education

The idea of love + a lost glove ÷ Hollywood = Popular marriage

Rape + smooth talk – a door and a cheekbone = Love at first sight

Shaky lips – stiff legs × oblong punch to abdomen = Commitment

Doña Cleta's samba ÷ mal de ojo + 2 joints = Calle Revolución, 11 P.M.

Chile powder soup^2 × onions & palm grease = Romantic guy

Baked bread × Zen thought – hands on her hips = One hand clap

Militarization of Brazil + Xingu extinction × deforestation = Money

Black boots × black lipstick gloss^3 × a knife = The corner

Crack + St. Martín Caballero × 2 needles = Blue skies

Man with briefcase – accent + big watch = Equal opportunity

Roped face × chained hands + free ankles = New democratic country

Ice + seashell × shaman hand over the mountain = PR Love letter

Castro Street × Wall Street ÷ 7 straight boulevards = Here

Two kilos of corn tortillas × roped luggage boxes = Latin promo

Bad accents^2 × 3 altar boy genuflections = High culture

Silent dinner ÷ stiff corset × big mustache = Dante's 13th ring

Snipped chicken head × chopped cactus + fried pork eye = Diploma

Foucault × lover with tiny red pants = Long walk to the clinic

Hard-core Chicana writer ÷ hard-core Latino writer = Fried race

June Journals 6-4-88

There are too many iron grids in California.

Literary grids are made of steel. The sturdiest of all iron fabrications. Who would think of literature as a fetter-cloak spread across the city, the chest, the tongue? Inmates have a nasty habit of stuttering. But, it is an act of empowerment. They interrupt themselves, stealing the occasion from the hollow-cheeked guard. Stuttering is a weapon. On the outside, for the Brown boy, the Down girl, the prolongation of our own sound is as defiant as acid. The question is, who speaks at all?

It Is Said

If you eat watermelon at night, you'll grow horns
If you listen to your eggs, you'll know who's after you
If you boil spinach with alcohol, you'll clear the house
If you keep dry bones, you'll dream of wild dogs
If you call a peccary, it will remember you
If you wear blue panties at an interview, you'll get a snow job
If you wear red briefs on the first date, you'll get the position
If you throw a chicken bone over your shoulder, he'll call
If you spit into his black olive twice, he'll choke on your name
If you memorize a license plate a day, you won't crash
If you wrap a green tie around your ankle, he'll give you the money
If you see three hummingbirds in a row, the world is yours
If you feed a fly for a week, you'll inherit property on Long Island
If you blow into a sock on Saturday, your nose will shrink
If you write seven words seven times, you'll find what you lost
If you drink violet water, you'll dream of witches
If you burn his hairs on a stove, he'll love your cooking
If you collect leaves and pennies, you'll get rich quick
If you follow people five times, they'll run from you
If you drink Yerba Azteca, you won't run out of bologna
If you stuff a golf ball into your bridal cake, you'll have a boy
If you say México backwards 100 times, you'll find Moctezuma's gold
If you do Zen while eating salami, you'll lose weight fast
If you sprinkle rosewater on your corns, your breath will sweeten
If you paste the Virgin on your dashboard, you'll make it to Tijuana.

How to Make World Unity Salsa

for Ray González,
George Kalamaras, & Thomas W. Ellis
—Catfish Butterfinger

Mash the pulp
Mash the pulp
Mash the pulp
Add a burned tomato & a rock of garlic
Add a burned tomato & a rock of garlic
Mash the pulp
In the black stone bowl
Mash the pulp
In the black stone bowl
Put your hand into it
Put your wrist into it
Put your shoulders into it
Mash the pulp in the black stone bowl
Mash the pulp in the black stone bowl
Put your hips into it
Put your hips into it
Char another chile
Char another chile
Mash the pulp
In the molcajete
Mash the pulp
In the molcajete
Just a pinch of salt
Just a pinch of salt
Pour in the soup from the tomato heart
Pour in the soup from the tomato heart
Now throw your head back twice

Now throw your head back twice
Mash the pulp in the molcajete
Mash the pulp in the molcajete
Mash the pulp in the molcajete
Yellow chile
Red chile
Green chile
Black chile
Brown chile wrinkled
White garlic
Black chile
Green chile
Red chile
Brown chile wrinkled
Yellow chile
Now throw your head back twice
Now throw your head back twice
Breathe baby
Breathe baby
Breathe baby
Breathe baby
Your fingers on the rock
Your palm on the stone
Your eyes on the inside
Your bones on the soul

Undelivered Letters to Víctor

#31

American originals, I repeat, then I think of time. Maybe time more than historical content or appropriation was the key to our missions. Maybe we wanted to simply acknowledge and conjure a crazy realignment with peoples and places cast out into a fabricated arena of temporal loss and jinxed distances, maybe we are at heart *time killers;* we want an exploded time, of things, ideas, and knowledge that we can feel at our side, inside of us, a complex chronos-fission, as though refracted in our mothers' tiny living rooms, our ringed hands, in thunderous accelerations, potholes, street signs, ranchero hats, Frida Rigoberta fists, tawdry publications and voices in Maya, rendings, rendijas, all sewn together, really, at random. We are rebel marauder Tiempo Pilots pillaging the day-to-day linear progression of Western time, of linear history that desires nothing more than to leave us all behind, accompanied only by its own guilt-processing time-keeping unit strapped to our "modern" psyche. And maybe, if we are here, unshackled, in this aura of the awakened present and its chambers of gnashing trade systems, global and virulent, in every maquila shoe, aesthete café cup and Madras shirt, we can now ask ourselves, well, what *is* foreign and distant? What belongs to a past that must not be ours, a slavery net that we left eons ago? How can our writing unlock time, snap us all into a plenum of actual realities? The year ends and a new one starts with these questions and riffs; the old Lochman Furniture store clock on Mission Street ticks again, then falls apart.

I, Citlalli "La Loca" Cienfuegos
SUTRA ON THE ADDITIONAL COUNTS OF SUFFERING

Late night:

Don't lissen to him and his rants,
I, Citlalli Cienfuegos burn alone—

What does he know? Knows nothing about my city of green winds and
reddish skirt lust lights over Market, reddish as in the fingers and rough elbows
of the teen Latinas in search of a diamond, let me say it this way, in search of a
kiss from the machine time-keeping unit. I stand alone in the rubble ground of
Tortilla Flats, warehouses of bound bedrooms, fastened tongue prisons, only
worker ants with anteater noses live here, a tropical blast from inside saves us,
at times, saves our sexual wasp-shaped torsos from additional counts of
suffering and loss and emptiness. Lissen to my night, lissen to my dance, my
black feet land on the street pyres of poets and word blower lamps hanging
from their tiny hands, their misshapen podiums. We gather, we frost, we foam
on the corner between rails and concrete, between condos and Plexiglas mini
fashion malls and barber shops colored in Huehuetenango orange stripes
mixed in with lilac. I desire this night, this stone worship night perfect for
thick leaves, storms, and Rio de Janeiro nakedness. My dark cinnamon thighs
feel the night heat, the night beat of crazy fingernails against the hotel brass
beds, the winos sucking in another forty-ounce bottle of prepaid love malt.
Who can count the kisses? Who can measure the slime thousands swiveling in
their tiny cots against oblivion and its agencies of corporate gangster howl?
I count the kisses and the shades that cut across the face in the last breath, the
last gaze of the hospital beds where the old and abandoned shrivel, here in
these sacred streets of blackish jazz talkative gutter shrunken apartment rooms
bejammed into everythingness and void. I, Citlalli Cienfuegos, mistress of
illegal flamencos in spasm and orgasm idioms—this is my cabaret. Who can
write it, who can trace its moist pubis?

La Marlene Grew Up in the Movimiento

Cuando era chiquita,
la llevaba a los sweats
up in DQU, Margarita tells me.

Even took her to the Sun Dance
one time,

allí andaba jugando
en pantalones de mezclilla,
with the chavalos.

All those Mecha meetings
in Sanjo too. In the front rows
of the community hall,

taking notes, running
around también.

We walked from Sanjo
to L.A. for the Moratorium
in '80 y no se quejó.

She took a step &
sat with me in the circle
con las comadres, when
we had our grupo de Florisong,

reading our first poemas
at my house on Pitcairn Street.

Things happened to her
when I got a divorce, Margarita pauses
looks up and begins again with more breath.
La Marlene lost faith in me, maybe
she lost faith in herself, I don't know
—she hurt too much.

It took her a long time,
she's had to catch up en la escuela.

Takes the SAT in April.
And now, mírala,
she's organizing readings
at El Rey, the Latino restaurant
on Cedar Street.

Esa Marlene,
grew up in el Movimiento.

June Journals 6-16-88

Fifteen years later at another institution in a much smaller room at Zapata Lounge, a Chicano dorm: no special lights, just an expensive mike. Javier Pacheco, Jorge González, (a Floricanto I survivor), Naomi Quiñónez, Alma Cervantes, Gloria Treviño, Rubén Martínez, Sesshu Foster do their stuff. L.A. comes across strong. Alma raps on gender roles and rollos with her *Vieja* poems. Margarita blisters the well groomed with her "Letters from the Horseshoe Murder." The invisible skull on the desolate hills of every California town opens its jaws of arranged imprisonments and decapitations. But, who listens?

Óyeme, Mamita
LETTERS ON ASPHALT, LETTERS ON COFFEE, LETTERS ON RAGS

Are we are the letters, Mamita? Óyeme, are we are the ones inside the words? Is this what you meant that night as you sat watching the Mexican tube and you turned to me? Just the other day I was talking to Víctor. He says he's not happy. Óyeme, did you hear that? Not happy. Look at him. He says he's going to Yosemite with his brothers, get away from all this stuff. Says he's going to hide out for six months in a shabby town nobody cares about. The letters are spittin' out diamonds now. Where did we start, was this our destination? Your lullabies, your corridos, that's where I started. Your stories about hard times in El Paso, Texas, as a young woman. I always lose it when I get romantic.

Undelivered Letters to Víctor

#10

1996 looms over me. I still think of José Antonio Burciaga, whose funeral we celebrated a few days before you went up to New York in early November. At Babaar's, we toasted to Tony—this is for José Antonio, we said as our faces slipped and blurred. He was just coming into his own, you said. After so many years making poetry, since '74 at the Centro Cultural de la Gente in San Jose, with his infamous makeshift priest outfit reading "Letanía en Caló" to the crowds, after all the *tertulias* and barbecues he used to have in Menlo Park and his "Drink Cultura" T-shirts, his "Last Supper" murals at Casa Zapata in Stanford and his irascible penchant for political cartoons and ascerbic journalism. His new book *Spilling the Beans* had just come out and then blam, just like that, cancer met up with him in a few quick merengue steps. His kindness stands out, it was his kindness, carnal, wasn't it? It was that simple—no rhetoric—kindness. Margarita Luna Robles got it in her to go up to Monterey and visit him on his last days. "Let's make him some enchiladas," she said with enthusiasm. Víctor, you should have seen Tony's face light up. "Just like my mom used to make them, El Paso style," Tony said, then we talked a while, he popped a dozen New Age snake powder pills, Cat's Claw, and we embraced each other. He was tired and lay down next to us. Around midnight, after Margarita and I left Monterey, as we passed through Hollister, two owls appeared over a telephone line. "Did you see that?" I asked Margarita. "He's not going to make it," she said in her typical straightforward voice. "Who is the second owl for?" I asked myself. Who? Who?

The second owl is for all of us. For Mario Savio who died a few days after you received your NBA medal, for his Free Speech time bomb set off decades ago (who will light it now?), for the Pocho-Che Collective and their attempt to create a new poetics—a Che Guevara face with palm tree hair superimposed on a Mission Street mesera, a "Tropicalifornia" and then the cultural centers along with a myriad of raza shops, teatros, and centros and casas that continue to work through their coups and power plays, echoing the power-shamble takeovers that blister through the city-system and the nation at large. The second owl is for the Red Nation writers too and their peyote orange juice vision of magic stone mothers and plumed-jacket fathers, you know what, Víctor, we came close to building Teotihuacán II, "city of the gods," in tiny farm towns and steely desolation rows. Close, baby. All that is gone now and in some way it stays with us, the way river ringlets keep on expanding into infinity. José Antonio is away now and his funny, political, bilingual, El Paso vibrations, that easy twang of spoken Chicano frontera jive, riffin' on borderlands realities, la migra, el chuko, las locas, el refín, gone too. And they remain as well. All the tasty molcajete raps we've been cooking for the last thirty years, the stuff no one published except ourselves, the stuff no one came to hear except ourselves and a few lefty wanna-be Latinos dissipates and re-emerges. This sounds religious and pious again, a bad Chicano habit.

My Plutomobile

Runs on ham hawks & bird grease
Runs on Gramshi's ashes in April
Runs on Saturn's sparkles
Runs on poems destroyed and reborn
Runs on Cuban drummers drinking mojitos
Runs on Satyricon rouge
Runs on the tiny kindness of Tarahumara grandmothers
Runs on Tosca steeples & red beans from Caguas
Runs on river rafts rolling to Bangladesh
Runs on Siva & Tatewarí at the same time
Runs on Mission Street into the Greek wines
Runs on a thumb print of Auschwitz
Runs on Elvis #2 by Warhol
Runs on Neruda's reconstruction of Chile
Runs on the lonesome dog howls of Barstow
Runs on the new secret seven-syllable pesticide
Runs on transvestite creativity & prune pie
Runs on pumpernickel tamales
Runs on Nuevo Laredo burlesque hip gestures
Runs on a Peruvian waltz
Runs on Borges the great encyclopedia swallower
Runs on the almighty mystery of sand
Runs on forged prison coupons
Runs on Mother Teresa's blue
Runs on the parallel lines of infinity & emptiness
Runs on my face fully realized before my birth
Runs on little Mexico in Buffalo, New York
Runs on Pinay Hula at Moonstone Beach
Runs reggae ragged
Runs on systemic counter evolutions

Runs on the gift of gab & seership

Runs on abalone voices

Runs on Che's last stroll in Buenos Aires

Runs on the trilobite shape of love

Runs on cashew butter fried salmon

Runs on Prague midnights

Runs on Vietnamese coconut water

Runs on student strike fevers in UNAM

Runs on a Nordic fjord

Runs on ozone in the saxophone

Runs on Selena's return

Runs on Arabic strings

Runs on Aymara potatoes

Runs on plutonium drums & a taste of bachata

Runs on the forgotten quipus of time

Runs on Einstein's first draft

Runs on the tight weave of a Guerrero straw hat

Runs in the solar winds of a Tzotzil huipil

Runs on posh & mezcal & pulque & chicha

Runs on the Iowa River with a dove call

Runs on metal flake cherry red & pineapple yellow

Runs on seven million Cantonese hello's

Runs on Afro-Peruvian belly mambos

Runs on the slave sugar prismatic in the sunken ships

Runs on Tel Aviv TVs

Runs on Transvaal liberation dances

Runs on the skin of a woman Ghana drum

Runs on free on free on free on free

June Journals 6-29-88

What is Mexico? Another fast stop for quasi-Beat U.S. middle-class poets to photograph themselves on a literary burro on their way to a Managuan book fair and a backyard hut experience for $800 so they can come back to their sanded-down desks somewhere overlooking the Bay Area and write a feeble twenty-page stroke of masturbations and distortions? Believe it or not, this is what is going on. Look around.

At the end of the month, Margarita and I will be going down to Tijuana for a writers' conference. We'll probably stop in L.A. and pick up Sesshu Foster, Rubén Martínez, and friends. I'll be looking hard. Everyone will be looking hard—I hope.

June Journals 6-5-88

Sunday.

There is an empty Foto-Mat store on 11th Street and San Fernando, next to San Jose State University's favorite laundry, a few feet from a 7/11 shop where most of the abandoned wanderers float from the halfway houses a few blocks away. Shriveled rose petals, cutout notes pasted on the iron grid windows, the best poem in the world taped to the door, laser printed. Here, in this brick cubicle, a young woman was stabbed to death recently trying to make a living by taking foto orders. When I read the poem on my way to teach my prison workshop I knew this was a *poem*. No publisher. No price necessary. No pages numbered. No sales clerk. No one waiting to see the poem or even hear the poem. But, it was the loudest poem, the most magnetic. A swollen tear, a naked vein, a deep green vine with the ability to turn its head in any direction, day or night and scream and breathe and live.

Simon Says

No bible in the tribe
keeps the culture alive.

While dreaming, eyebrows float
as sheep grazing on cinnamon cliffs.

The hand contains the maps
to three dimensions:
      health
      friendship
      fear

Banjo plucking imitates
upside down rain dance.

The eye that sees without light
sees all night.

Discover the valve for kindness
between the throat and the thumb.

A leaf and a wave have the same arc
between the stem and the curl.

Honey is the tears
of ancient ancestors forgiving us.
Wind is the skin
of the universe.
One hand clapping happens all the time.

Undelivered Letters to Víctor

#4

I've been away for a while. But I never leave this tropical cement speckled with finger polish and Pinoy rice. Café la Bohème boils with Mexicanos who think this is Veracruz where you can tap your dish with a teaspoon to send messages across the room, they hunch their Thrift Mart rags on their back, smoke deep Winstons, hook their jaws and order another hot jasmine tea, read the *Bay Guardian* like they're washing their hands in licorice water. They smell their hands and smoke again, talk without words and in the morning they line up on Army or as they say nowadays César Chávez Boulevard, looking sad and mean and melancholy, they stand up on old army and wait for the job, la troka, that will haul them in bundles to a lawn, a backyard, a garage with a broken old Buick or simply to a yard of freakish bushes and branches epileptic and hardened by trash and the boom-crash of wild neglect.

—

A Poet's 2027 Odyssey Backpack Instructions

Do it on the road, Red
Feed it on the branch, Beaulah
Knead it on the berry, Bobo   ·
Braid it on the forest, Freydo
Lose it on the water, Waldo
Hear it on the feather, Fifi
Gold it on the shade, Samuel
Slam it on the rose, Rosa
Pull it on the wine, Winston
Cord it on the salt, Sibyl
Riff it on the bone, Balthazar
Run it on the fender, Freddi
Fold it on the lamb, Leroi
Frost it on the ear, Everardo
Clamp it on the night, Néstor
Clip it on the atom, Adam
Toss it on the first, Fanny
Sing it on the steeple, Steph
Drop it on the spirit, Spiro
Jam it on the pollen, Pablita
Groove it on the wire, Wilson
Let it lay on the leaf, Leon
Be it on the Honey, Honey

Undelivered Letters to Víctor
#9

I want to rock in Tede Matthew's America and his Hula Palace—remember Tede Matthews? Tede out-gay talking about Nicaragua, doing the reading series at Modern Times? Tede working hard through AIDS, through the pain and the end, with gaunt face, febrile fingers, and starry eyes? Tede's drawn face calls and his clear eyes peer through me. Battles, missions, random intersections, chaos, time and culture boosters, explosions; I want writing to contain all this because we contain all this—is this closer to what you mean by saying we are Americanos? Is this your mission? You know Víctor, I am going to say it—no more movements, nothing about lines or metaphors or even about quality and craft; you know what I mean?

Ten Still Lives

Man flying over bridge with orange sunset on shirt
Chain-walk through the mainline with ragged cuffs against red ankles
President at banquet with sheep in background
Mayor naked on purplish pillow with cocaine dish
Maid in master's kitchen with fast butcher knife
Ditch diggers on Broadway with three-piece suit sociologists
Girl in morgue freezer with boyfriend's blue ribbon on neck
Forty-eight stitches over thorax with two mortadella torpedos on the side
Husband in cheap hotel with mini-truck smoking
Two breasts touching with two breasts touching

June Journals 6-13-88

I am looking across the table. Margarita Luna has just finished organizing a Chicano Floricanto literature festival at Stanford University. Marylin M. taped it on a Nagra. We've been working on a film for quite a while on the story of Chicano Park, an odd spot of ground underneath a slab of concrete stretching from the coast of San Diego to Coronado Island where high school choirs visit ivory hotel lobbies on Christmas; Chicano Park—an obscure patch of land taken from the gloved hands of the city and the highway patrol in the early seventies.

Floricanto Literature Conference, a beginning for Chicano poets coming together on November 14th and 15th in 1973 at USC. Óscar Z. Acosta, Alurista, Tomás Rivera, Teresa Palomo Acosta, Alejandro Murguía, Omar Salinas to name a few, mostly men. What really happened? We pulled out colored scarves, a feverish clown, Goya with tinted spectacles. I sang with my guitar. We spoke of Amerindia, our new nation gilded with the color of our skin and with the deep touch of our grandmothers. But no one dared speak of grandmothers. Chicanas did. Men uttered the priestly psalms of an Indian Paradiso, now to be reconjured. Except for Z. Acosta. "Put out the lights. I don't want this to be recorded," he said standing in silhouette. I was angry. I wanted to see another clown. But he was a clown of darkness. So he read chapter 14 from *Revolt of the Cockroach People,* his novel in progress—without light; the story of a vato who is hooked by the cops and strangled in his cell with the magical tie of arranged suicide. A beginning of our sound: Goya with and without spectacles. Fabrication and Madness. Men in line signing books.

Steppin' into Power in the Age of Plutonium, the Super-Right, & Other Explosives
UCB Regents Fellow Lecture, February 4, 1997

What does it mean to step into power?
What are the key questions of our time?
What time are we living in, has time changed at all?
Why do we want power in the first place?
Power from where

the earth that moans from pollution, quakes
from its own tectonic blasts? the earth divided?
the earth abandoned, the earth reclaimed
through armed struggle,
through one more war? Power through ledgers,

thru words,
thru flesh.

Power from the nation?
Can we truly respect its borders?

Borders made with genocide, occupation,
oppression, and colonialism,
old words, university words—
genocide,
occupation,
oppression,
and colonialism—

there is something real, isn't there, in those university words,
outside the academy, the words might be

food,
water,
mother,
daughter,
body,
house,
blood,
oxygen,
light,
hunger,
over here,
carnala.

Can we truly respect its borders,
these nation borders?

Power from organizations, assemblies,
collectives, institutions. Perhaps here the question is,
do we qualify?

That seems to be the question
most of our institutions ask today.

Do you qualify, do you meet our criteria,
do you have proper papers, beliefs, ideologies,
shape, form, values, language, affiliation?

Do you qualify?
Or are you unqualified?
You may not belong with us?

Power from what point?
From the individual?

Why is it that the individual carries so much weight,
if the individual is only one and the group is many?
Why isn't the collective our goal, our task, our dream?

In this country, the group does not exist,
since we are merely individuals, thick with individual meanings,
prowess, accumulation, direction—ambition.
and the group—an interesting aside.
Individuals like to talk about groups.
Do we really know what a group is?
What it means to give of our individual self to the larger,
hungrier, more painful collective self—the group. Whose group?
You see? Individual ownership sneaks in its pungent nose.

What myth shall we embrace?

The myth of liberation?
The myth of language?
The myth of diversity?
The myth of learning?
The myth of artistic devise?
The beautiful myth of change? ·
The myth of Goddess?
The myth of Culture?
The myth of Family?
The myth of Body?
The myth of Love?
The myth of Sexuality?

Will this myth suffice?

Can we live without myth? I mean,
the urban secular nonflavored, sanitized,
dispassionate myths; surely no one here truly participates
in a visceral system of ordeals and visions and givings
and sharings that at any moment can shatter

the people's being and society if that person missteps
& abuses power?

No matter how many piercings, tattoos, hollers,
mosh pits we may delve into, we have the nasty habit
of bouncing back into our current miasma of meaninglessness,
petty frames of violence from all directions.

Power from form: oh, yes form—
the snake oil of the postmodern.

Change the form,
spit on the form,
burn the form,
go formless,
why not?
go formless,
come on you can do it.

A little bit of form-resistance
will get you places! So many forms,

Xtian forms, educational forms, forms for lovingness, healing forms,
Deepak Chopra forms in one easy three-minute step, forms for men, forms
for women, hetero forms, yeah, they make for really cool targets, homo-
forms, try 'em, see what happens, conceptual forms, theory forms, more
flesh forms, familia forms, forms for a big bad brave new crisis, therapy
forms, Zen forms, excuse me there are no Zen forms, listening forms,
corporate forms, there are too many already can someone stop making
them so we can choose one or two, ritual forms, forms for humans and
animals and plants, language forms, sprechen Sie Spanish?

187
209
277
2007?

Power in the age of plutonium?
What can a poet do against nuclear warheads,
what can a book or a study or a chant or a horoscope
or a report or a piece of paper or a letter or a poem,
did I say poem,

what can art do,
what can you do, me,
us, them, against us
and against them
do against nuclear warheads?

You still want power?
For the right, left, middle,
blurred power? Power of the weak
Power up, power in, empowered
powerful, powerhouse, whose house?

what if you live in a shack
made out of newspaper
and toilet rolls & Butterfinger wrappers
for curtains? Hydroelectric power?

Visit Chiapas and Guatemala
the hydroelectic prostitutes of this continent,
where are the pimps? That is the question
where are the power pimps? Or is the word
energy?

Is that a more modern word?
—energy?
I know I can't say love, right?
I know I can't say compassion, right?
I know I can never say patience, of course, of course.
I know I cannot say intimate things,
intimate things, intimate terms

intimate gestures, even worse then language
a gesture?
Someone said love and got canned, got aced
someone said compassion and got butchered
someone said patience
and got laughed out of the workshop.

What if we lost the term power.
What if we went nonverbal all the way.

Can we stop the noise. The bomb in the box
The blood on the wheel, the DNA chart, dots—
rectangles & ink, the guilty verdict
the plastic explosive on the tip of our tongue?

There is the matter of fear, I know.

homophobic fear
mexiphobic fear
asiaphobic fear
jewphobic fear
afrophobic fear
color & class & ass fear
europhobic fear, age-grade fear
indiaphobic, no I don't think so—
some group took care of the Indians already
but the fear is there, they keep on coming back.

Shall we destroy the fear,
the paranoia?
Feelings:
who cares about such tiny, stupid, wishy washy tendrils.
Of course, there is one more thing about feelings and fears:

unfinished business, past traumas—
the holocaust that continues past memory

the concentration internment camps, that no-no Braille
inside our eye, the broken treaties, the Trail of Tears,
the Vietnam reflex poppin' another sugar
glazed donut with a handful of aspirinas & a zip gun in San Jose—

more traumas
inside the purse, and the hip pocket, the acetabulum crushed, ripped bodies
        floating in
the basement slime, death jams us when we are having our gifelte fish
        w/ two stanzas of Szymborska, gimlets with guacamole-smeared ribs
        over rice and acorn squash—

power
power power creeps into
all of our conversations, our lives.

What does it mean to step into power? What are the key questions of our
time? What time are we living in, has time changed at all? Why do we want
power in the first place? Power from where? Made from what?

June Journals 6-25-88

The check I bounced was for $208. My buddy, Alfonso S., did the design and layout for Víctor Martínez's first book, *Wrecking Them Back*. I feel like telling Vic to forget it. Ain't got the dough. Shit. Another good book down the great tar pit of Chicano scrawl. Now what? I know Víctor has something cooking in these poems. *Zyzzyva* just published "National Geographic" in their summer issue. And now, even that micro-crack in the North Americani Universe of Chicano Chance is over. Víctor has the biggest voice in Califas at this very second. But it is leashed. Or perhaps it gains fetters when it is published? I think so. This is the tightrope we walk. Wait for Juan Godot to publish our stuff or just let it roam, loose-toothed, and angry at readings, rallies, tables, and sidewalks? What shall it be: North American Literary Order that is "Craft" or Sabotage, our openness without official gatekeepers, word gendarmes?

I told Alfonso I would pay him in cash. He said the check was redeposited by his bank. I wish my bank would do that once in a while.

Undelivered Letters to Víctor
#38

Perhaps the notion of being American is off center—there is no center,
I guess that's the thing. AIDS is not a line or a metaphor or an iambic
construct, or a national artifact, a session on meter. You can't lean it on
quasi-nationalisms, or Aztec sloganeering. You can't prop it up as a
mariachi Rimbaud gone Latino wearing a vest of alienation and a paisley
button that reads "Peasant Power!" It is not enough to go about ranting
"qualified" ethnic know-how, "minority" bombast, harpooning dead
islands, manifestos and poets—that boat ride is over, baby. Any flirtations
with "language" aestheticism sprinkled with a taste of retro bohemia will
not pull us through. Language seeks linear time and history, it wants to
appear monumental, greater than us. In a sense, language wants to ignore
the facts; now I am sounding Tibetan, I feel like I am talking about the
wheel of illusions. These are facts, for now: the mottled flesh sheet of viral
invasion, global and phantasmagoric, these facts break through our mouse
hole, our underground, our missions, our sacred bundle of wired words.
At this very second AIDS gnaws away at our pretensions, at our internal
cellular texts; this event alone, by itself, without further elucidation, unites
us, moves us, informs us, gives us death and spirit. Blood writing: the last
manifesto and true axis of this new millennium. The ante has never been
so high for us. To write "ethnic folk drama" is not sufficient, to join the
Hispanic Movimiento Advertising Machine, whose main function is to pat
its own rhetoric on the back and spawn a new generation of "melting pot"
ventriloquists, is out of the question, to huddle around a literary agent who
tells us to keep it current, PC, and racy, to install a refurbished fem Virgen
de Guadalupe over the ruins, once again, is not sufficient, to stay in the
"color" game, the hetero-sex gang, and never unite with sisters and brothers
will annihilate us, we got to match wits with the RNA Gila Monster inside
of us, we got to keep close to all of our lives as they suffer, as they bleed all
around us, the mission is on, Vic—I am wandering off, again, I know.

Sonny, Rudy, René, & Me
Escondido, mid-fifties

At the park.
With Levis thick as tree bark and white T-shirts tucked in for the fifties look.
Zapatos, woven with string shoelaces. We sit on a rail. Our arms around the
stillness, the soft bones of our shoulders. This is Sonny who sang "Silent
Night" to a charred iguana, in the fields next to a busted house. This is El
Rudy, older than the rest of us. No one knows where he lives. Only the
sadness streaked across his face, a split shadow. René smiles. Short and
strong at seven. Cuffed. Rudy could have been my older brother. I make a
clown face. The fence behind us crosses its *X*'s. One hundred *X*'s for each
one of us.

I, Citlalli "La Loca" Cienfuegos
SUTRA ON THE CATEGORY MAKERS

Don't look at me for the answers, do not lift your feeble fuzz pens, your loaf of electricity, your last butter stick, that shab ointment you call your language, your meaningfulness. Who? I ask you again, who knows my city, my archipelago, these flat board tenements in liquor light, in see-through Spandex gauze of the lover gone mad? I stand alone on my boulevard, with my small audience of category makers, not word tuners or word flutterers or word hissers or word twisters, I said category makers. I am the idea, I am the concept, I am the liquid syrup that messes with the machine's objectives. Lissen to my webbing moan, my oboe throne, these pipes on my back, these lacquer faces in fiery spark, these curled neon baby-faced cloud singers, these children with old arms and ancient blood and swollen groin and belly and womb, the ones who light candles on Potrero Hill rain, the ones who climb under the moon in Bernal Heights and who cling to the leaves, the strays, and sing again to turn to sol to sing and they are Velázquez and they are Allende and they are Menchú monster girls with the mascara of fright futures and disaster wishers, they are in formation, they are tapping against your glassy palace at this very second.

Tío Chente Brings Ancient Coins from China

for you, Tío,
you had it right
from the beginning

That's your tío Chente, mamá would tell me paging through this old album.
Ése es, the one with a sombrero de paja selling paintings in New York, en los
veintes. El artista in the family, the one who made juguetes out of wood in
El Paso. Yo no trabajo para nadie, he would tell my abuela Juanita Martínez
de Quintana. So he made painted toys out of cracked 2×4's. My mamá and
my aunt Lela, the one destined for solitude, would sand them down.
    Saw him last about twenty years ago. Venía con beret, saco de
burgundy stripes. Looked like Dalí or a French chef. Hadn't changed much
since '66 when he told me to drop out from San Diego High. We were living
on 11th Street apartment #2. Block down from Pearson Ford. Join up with
me, Juan, he said, what are you doing here? I'll teach you sculpture, the old
kind maybe you can help me restore the churches in Balboa Park—learn silk
screen, oils. I had been to his second-story room on "B" Street, a makeshift
cavern. Tubes of Thalo Green dragging S's into the titanium white, red-
caked oils on his breakfast wedge-table.
    In the tub, blackened paper, shapeless, drowned in brown water.
A hazy oil copy of a Goya woman, slanted on his broken bed, thick pearl
smoke negligee, chalk breasts. Sculpture? I said. Pulled out a charcoal sketch
of my hand—stood there, with the paper in the air. Remember him now,
Tío Chente, the same emptiness and freedom in the corners of his lips, my
mother silent in the kitchen folding quesadillas with jamón. I am doing
murals, he says, en las iglesias. Raising feria for los Indios Kickapoo. Shows
me a wrinkled article, scribbled notes. Empties his bolsas, gives my jefita a
blotched bag of square coins from Japan, Korea, China, Singapore, the
Philippines. Here, he tells her, maybe you can sell them. Comes to me
again—Tío Chente, de ochenta años, tilts his head to one side, Well, tell
me, Juan, what are *you* doing now?

Notes on Other Chicana & Chicano Inventions
for all middle-school teachers
& bilingual teacher aides

Like I said,
Cilantro aftershave

Hominy &
peanut butter burritos

Sanwishes
de sardinas con ketchup

(I am not going
to mention the lowrider,
actually created in Tijuas in the forties,
José Samuel Flores told me—
mecánico de primera)

Huevos for empacho & mal de ojo
Plantillas for bad fiebres
(make sure you use manteca de puerco)
Bendiciones for a good day
Migajón for enojo

Arroz con leche with pasas
Ponches de huevo con canela

The art of eating Vicks VapoRub with your dedos
The art of sucking an egg w/o breaking the shell
The art of splashing yourself with alcohol & ruda

Sobadas
Aceitadas

Hueseras & curanderos
Mamberos & merenguidas

Tepaches & tardeadas
Lunadas & barbekiadas
"Jalapeños in a Circle K bag"
(you can use this phrase
when you sing the Twelve Days
of X-mas at your in-laws, Cuñao
Louie wrote it)

How to wear your khakis high up to your chin
w/o chopping your nachas
How to roll up your catholic pleated skirt
& look favorable
How to make braids out of anything,
even masa, or calcetines
How to take a two by four
and make skates, surfboards
How to make parches & remendadas
& empanadas de camote
How to make velas take
your wishes to the universe
How to make salsa with stones,
fire and boxwood
How to make a chicken say, por favor,
sí señor, sí señora
How to feed the cat estek con papas,
refrieds & espinaka
How to bang on the roof to get
the tapa de la olla down
How to wear your hair high up
so it looks like a tipi.

The word *machaca*
The word *fayukero*
The word *garabato*
The word *chuchulukos*
The word *brekas*
The word *chorreada*
The word *apestosidad*
The word *huevonetes*
The word *achicopalado*
The word *mixtiada*
The word *berruga*
The word *estinche*

Code words like *caldo,* like *pelotas,* like *ojos de rata*

Phrases like
You better wash those dishes Juan,
or I'll give you a wamazzo.
Phrases like
I said, you better wash those trastes
o te tuerzo el hociko boy.
Phrases like
You better not hang around with that bola
de mariguanos o arranco that branch off
el árbol y te curo las sentaderas.
Phrases like
Keep on painting your carota de chankla
like that & you're gonna get granotes
the size of a calabaza, you hear,
escuincla?

Undelivered Letters to Víctor
#17

I'm livin' in Fresno, now, you know, like you used to; I ask my friends, how should I know about the Mission District, the writers? Because you were there broda, right? You were there when the gettin' was good, when they took down the Shaft on Mission Street and put up the Centro Cultural de la Mission in 1977, you know what it's all 'bout, carnal, they say. Let's talk about other things, I mumble, sometimes I prefer solitude, peek at what fire still burns in me or is it iciness? I want to write this open closed thing, this

Rwanda Chiapas in our living rooms,
this full empty street with anti-graffiti artists,
this city cutting through the plutonium, the last tropic, the one
with love and nothingness tearing through its palm-shaped heart.

Ejotes con Mayonesa
San Jose, summer, 1985

Rolling down the grapevine. Highway 5 from Rialto to San Pancho—past
Denny's next to the Exxon station—got hungry for my mother's guisados.
You know, huevos ahogados en tomate, espinacas con chile on a hard day
old hand-made tortilla de harina, huevos fritos con valoney w/ a side of
brown chipotles. Simple ensalada too. You take a cucharada grande of
mayonesa slam it on a plato of cooked ejotes.

Orange Stop on 99

In my jefito's baby blue Army Dodge grilled troke, 1954

Ain't nothing better, than pulling over—after the pizca in Fresno, on the
way to the next one in Delano. On a hot day leave the troke running, snap
off a half dozen of the grower's naranjas for the sweet road ahead. ¿Qué no?

Undelivered Letters to Víctor
#11

Just want to congratulate you in some way that makes sense, although congratulations sounds ill-fated, maybe I'll just call you and we'll talk about your National Book Award. You been hiding in your apartment for so long, this sudden media tidal wave about you and your book makes me laugh. That's all you do now, right? Sign books, appear on television, sign more books, do a radio show, swallow a lozenge before the stage manager counts you down. But you stayed true to form when you denied a contract for your next book without writing a single page. "I didn't want that kind of pressure on my head," you said. Órale, carnal, true to form. I want to write a novel on the Mission, you told me at Babaars. I know it will be ferocious. Thing is, what will you say?

I, Citlalli "La Loca" Cienfuegos

SUTRA ON THE NINTH SUN

They—the category babies, know my name. Call me Citlalli "La Loca," in
this wind. Bring me a mango in thrombosis, the catch of the rice day, the
net bag full of ocean shuffle and asphalt scribble, the Ninth Sun is upon us,
here in these flat boards of rock roses and barbed butterflies. My city boils
in the velvet shade. My city sings for its return to my little womb house, my
gypsy songs smuggled from Chiapa de Corso, from el Rastro in Madrid, the
alley is my necklace, the boulevard is my guitar. Sing then and howl again,
tiny Ginsberg Lorca California with your bubble cock, tiny Frida unto hip-
hop bongo curbs and howl again, here next to me, to my breast, come close
and shiver with daybreak starry winds, call upon me, recline your charcoal
nipples, your rough hair and let us walk alone and together, stroll and break
through the levers, the gizmo worldwide net of bluenothing, pronounce me
free, I am Citlalli Cienfuegos, I stand alone in a Socrates Tortilla Flats trial.
No—it is my trial I am speaking of, it is my sedition I am referring to, it is
my hanging you are laughing at, it is my brain you are swimming through,
it is my parade in liquor malt hosiery and maquila corporate garters, my face
astounds you and lures you and mixes you into another life, presses your
countenance and identity and modernity, I said come, I said let us gather
alone and separate, let us spin flamey, guard the pyres ten feet high, let us
make the now noise tambourine festival public, throw away the skin lamp,
the bushes of shame dimes. Lissen close, come up to my dress halfway
down, feel my belly, hot and stormy, my face, pocked and diamond-eyed,
ready to please and swing one more delirium in—you.

Cry Like a Man

Days after my mother died, Margarita said, "She was all you had." No
brothers, no sisters, no father, believe me—hadn't even thought about it.
I was busy with the veils in my head, the poetry-in-the-community thing.
Just went on with teaching at De Anza Community College until the day
I came home and she couldn't breathe. I was numb, stonelike inside after I
left the San Jose Hospital on 14th Street. 11:45 P.M., a Thursday. Last
Thursday in Julio, 1986. Margarita said, "You know, Ed Hayashi? El japonés,
the one always saying 'Fuck this, fuck that at the office,' you know, that
tough vato who wears sandals to work? You should've seen him, the day his
jefita passed away, in front of everybody, he cried like a baby." One night
later, I invited a few friends. Barlow and my tía Albina whom I hadn't seen
in years, since she moved to Santa Clara when my tío Beto was still living.
Each one spoke in the narrow circle. Barlow read a poem & it was the first
time I ever heard my tía Albina talk about my mother. When it was my
turn, next to my mother's ashes, at the open center believe me, camaradas,
I began to cry. This was my beginning.

June Journals 6-6-88

When my mother died I discovered a small address book. I was going
over her things, still wanting to hold her, somehow. I opened the book and
I found notes that my mother had written in the early fifties when we were
moving in and out of ranches in Southern California. My dad, Felipe, was a
farmhand and his odd jobs took us into the abandoned terrains of Carlsbad,
Ramona, Escondido, Lake Wolfer. One afternoon he brought home a pail of
perch, his salary for the day. On another occasion he hauled in a sack of
sweet potatoes and a crate of avocados.

Mom's notes speak of arrivals and departures. Things about me having a
cold or in an office waiting for a welfare check. In other sections she has
proverbs or lines for songs in Spanish, or phrases she remembers from a
novel she read when she was a girl. There is no fancy title other than
"Addresses" in gold leaf—arrivals and departures. What really influences a
writer? Addresses? No chapters? No audience? Lucha Quintana, my mother,
is the writer that influences me. Because it is all about deep connection,
about deep nurturance and about deep loving. How can there be real
relationships without these?

The Cat My Mother Cradled

At sixteen, at midnight they came knocking. Said my father had died of complications. My mother shuddered. Fell. Something dropped inside of her and grew above us. A tiny flame of sweetness and black. For years, in that wild shadow, she smoked and kissed a stray that crossed our window.

Avenida Constitución, Tijuana

My tío Ferni's idea—wanted me casual. Welfare chavalo south of San Diego, third-grade drapes by the local sastre on Avenida Constitución. What was I?

A chopped-down drop of Pedro Infante, a Santo Niño de Atocha with farm shoes, calcos spit-shined and tramos lined with English Cashmere? 1956. Maybe 1957. I saw myself for the first time, in this electric sleeve, from the forties—when Fernando strolled with my Tía Aurelia. See him lock his arm around her waist. Con sombrero y traje negro down a narrow bank. En la capital. Years before he earned his position as a laundry Mexican, smiling king of starched cotton.

El Teatro Reforma (con Clavillazo & Queso de Puerco
Tortas on the Side during Intermission, circa 1959,
Tijuana, Baja California)
for Lauro Flores, days of El Bujazán

El Reforma, the new teatro in Tijuas.

What you gotta do: hit La Victoria panadería ten minutes early. Pack a bag
of virotes and pan dulce, you know—campechanas, conchas de chocolate,
orejas, empanadas de piña, cocos. Don't forget the queso de puerco (rub it
on your nose, a gasolina con perfume de Woolworths). Clavillazo rolls out
behind the curtains wearing his famous canoe hat and flag-coat with pillow
pockets. Don't forget the aguacates and a bouquet of wild cilantro. Pura
vida Clavillazo says as my mother breaks out the bolsa, splits the bolillo and
spreads the aguacate on her legs. You don't have to worry about nothing.
When you turn around to slip in the torta everyone does the same.

The Red-Striped Accordion I Never Played

Was on the black & white TV box.

When I went to the parque, the Escondido Accordion Club played. Eight dollars for the lessons, the director said. I raised my hands up to my side and played the flannel cloth over my ribs. From a distance, my shirt stretched and burned. And my hands, so fast. You wouldn't notice.

La Momia Azteca Always Followed Me across the Border While I Hid Madero Whiskey in My Cowboy Boots (Late Night Traffic)

Póntela en las botas. Put it in your boots.
Tío Ferni said. En la línea. He revved his '53 Plymouth on the way back from El Bujazán where they just showed La Momia. As we hit San Diego, 17 miles north the city opened its necklace of yellow coals. Madero. La Momia. My face angled in the night. Lights, so many flame-lights wrapped around the tiny pool-shaped mirror.

Love the Victim Harder Than You Love His Killer
a Velorio

Margarita prays
for her 22-year-old brother, Ricky—
run over, late night, by a full truck.
Next to a 7/11.

Sometimes, from a small envelope
she pulls out his broken bones,

or she finds his torn fingers
at the bottom of a cup of coffee.

"Then they kicked him, then they stabbed him
then pierced him, front to back
with a meat cleaver," I listen to her.

I listen to her.
See her wringing her own hands like rags
thirteen years after Ricky's death.

Todos los vatos
took a turn, she says.

Had a kick-down good time
& then, they ran away.
To get high, click on the boom box.

Keep on listening.

None of 'em got time.
No one said a thing.

Tiny barrio killers.
Hard kings to themselves. Hard
kings to the young chavalos.

Look at how they love their mirrors, in their own
blood-filled silence. Look at their stiff faces.

Don't ask me why they killed him.
Don't ask me if they were abused.
Don't ask me if they were loaded.
Don't ask me about their broken fathers.
Don't ask me, camarada. Please don't ask me.

Ask yourself
who are your heroes?

Ask yourself
Do you know how to love? Walk down.

Down there, by your house.
The night is wet with victims,
year in year out.

Chican@ Literature 100

First of all, you are not going to find this stuff at the mall, in one of those flashy pendejada shops. Maybe you'll have to quiet yourself down, listen to yourself, try pintura for a few days, maybe weeks take rainy walks, make small mirrors rake the front yarda, listen to the rake speak, do a mandado for your abuelita if she still lives (do it w/o berrinches) dig up black dirt on the trail in the forest, carry twisted wood and leave it at the edge of the road with good words between you and the squirrel behind the trees, go back and find the seed-voices, the ones that raised you, the letters that arrived with your red-green spirit, the ancient songs way deep inside.

How to Enroll in a Chicano Studies Class

Spring, '68,
struttin' down Westwood

You don't know how good I felt when I saw a whole grupo of raza at
UCLA in '68 from barrios like Wilmas, Norwalk, Whittier, Bakersfield (and
Chicano Studies was still a dream). We had rushed the chancellor, told him
he had to share the pastel, give us some slack (of course we stormed the
administration, a la brava). Puro chocolate, at last—el Cricket combing
his hair into the shape of a goose outside the chemistry building. Speaking
out: la Adelaida & la Gloria M.—una güera y la otra prieta, una en teatro, la
otra pre-law. Never felt so de aquéllas, even when the frats put up a sign
pledging students. Sign said: "No Zapatas Allowed." No problem, me & el
Edda, Rana, and Monsivais took care of it. A baby molotov, at midnight—
the East L.A. method. Good thing it didn't go off. But, they got el mensaje.
We invented Chicano Studies, con manos limpias en las mañanas,
demanding our rights (this sounds old now but we did demand our rights).
With our language, our home-poems, our long walks and fasts for justice—
Delano, Sacra, Coachella. I can say this. This was our starting point, a
healing red across the borders churned with brown clay, rain clouds, open
arms, yerbas, a single leaf from the eucalyptus, for each one of us. This is all
you need. Breathe in, breathe out, this green wind, makes you strong.

How to Be a Warrior for the Aztlán Liberation Army (ALA)

Didn't have the eight track

but I had the rest—

Three Roses pomade, stiff khakis, greased head, Levis as hard as ceramic pants, cardboard boxes instead of suitcases (even when I went to the university orientation), a penchant for tragedies, especially those performed by Pedro Infante in *Nosotros los pobres* or Buñuel's *Los olvidados,* was in love with Sarita Montiel, the Spanish actress who starred in *La violetera,* wanted the long honey of her reddish hair pouring down her back & María Victoria, her manly voice and fish-shaped black steel dress, ate biznagas for breakfast, roasted chicken feet with cocido for dinner as I gawked at Lawrence Welk with my mom, wore navy blue beanies and navy blue turtle necks to high school thinking I was a Post-Chicano Beatnik, even though I was the only one who thought that, sometimes I would wear my Day-Glo green short sleeves & my tight silver-lined black hustler sport coat bought on pawnshop row, 5th Street, San Diego (for junior high graduation). Still wear it. For lonche, in the early years—tomate and butter sanwishes or sanwishes de sardina with a tiny green and yellow can of pineapple juice (me & George Escalera were the only Chicanos at Lowell Elementary who carried giant chrome can openers), these days I make the best Chicano antipasto: sardinas coloradas either in mustard sauce or tomates with french bread, diced jalapeños, cilantro, and relish, tastes like the Vietnamese tortas they make in Sanjo, in Little Saigon. Every Halloween I smeared my face with brown oil, made big holes on my clothes so I could look like a pirate or a hobo, the only roles I knew how to play and the cheapest, wait a minute, I did have a radio, a twelve-transistor box that I took to Mission Beach in San Diego with Heredia, scouting for chavalas & his famous primo Hugo who said he knew about French Lit. Always wore flat tops, Mohawks, or butches, now it doesn't matter, 'cuz my head actually is square, my stepchildren laugh at it, I feel good about these ondas, there's more too, like when I used to raise my hand during the Pledge of Allegiance, in first grade—Central Elementary because I had questions & when I sang tenor in high school in a barbershop quartet, puffed shirts with garters on the upper sleeves, this is how I made myself speak out, how I waxed my soul, in this style, put a teatro together in '70, a Puerto Rican wrapped up in aluminum foil supposed to represent nuestra opresión, then, Troka, a conga group from Fresno, in '82 spent thousands to make it to Boston where we sang a Dion piece at MIT as an encore. For a couple of years walked around sin calzones, in manta pants, huaraches, or thongs, drinking purified water, carried in a small glass jar—tied to my turquoise belt, the one from Veracruz, I was on a search, my heart was open, talking about El Movimiento, using the words *espíritu* & *liberation,* ask my camaradas, they know and who knows what I'll do next.

I, Citlalli "La Loca" Cienfuegos
SUTRA ON THE MACHINE HOLE

Do you understand without so much understanding, without so much, you inside the machine hole, you, can you hear, yeah you, the one inside the groove cable, inside the mayoral plasma filters, come out now, it is too dark for them to see you, speak a little, say a little word, a Nahuatl fragment sound, touch the frets, strum a little Cakchiquel, perk up in the circle, who can tell, who knows, maybe you will awaken soon, your Morisco eyes will open for my mirror breasts, take me now, come on, you and me, alone, on this water street, outside the center, the big club of wretched loss, ripped from the earth, my raft is behind me, it is ready, the waters are rising, the lights and bells are flickering, step in and welcome the half-bitten moons, the easy dreamers tapping your shoulders, come now, do not lose your way.

Vietnam Veterano Special (with Aspirins & White Powdered Donuts)

for Charley, the Last Chicano Kong,
San José, Califas, 1986

Charley picks me up in his off-white '79 Celica. (Margarita needs our '74 B-210 to drop off Marlene at the new junior high school.) He lives by the Sanjo hospi, a few bloques near the halfway houses.

"Man, you shudda seen Bangkok in '69, ése." Chews on five aspirinas for his high blood-pressure problema. "& one day, ése, we got ambushed, chingao, I knew it too. Cause I lost my virgencita that day. Walking the point, I felt my neck and she wasn't there." Takes a long swig de la Coka. "Up the loma, had to blow out a gook. Shit, he was waiting for me con un AK-47 on the side of the pinchi hill." Drinks down the Coka, pulls a dona through the cellophane, starts the engine. "Then, check this, ése, this Cheekan got into it with an Okie 'cuz, the Okie drank all the Kool-Aid while the rest were on patrol. The real cura is . . ." he slows, swerves a little, and touches the left side of his face. "The real cura is that I blew out my eye practicing on a bazooka. I'm workin' on a novela about the whole enchilada," he pauses again, "about the soldados from Corcoran—the ones that came back, you know. Man," he says, throws more aspirinas down the hatch, "we all took the TWA, carnal." Las donas look good, I take one and ask—what TWA? "The Wrong Airline, candy-ass!" We get on 280, head toward Cupertino, De Anza College. Buildings & pieces of palm tree melt across the windshield. Charley teaches Chicano literature, I teach cross-cultural communication.

Taking a Bath in Aztlán

for Yermo & Susana Aranda,
early San Diego Movimiento pioneers, 1973;
for Rod Ricardo Livingstone

Fast for three days on arroz and sweet tortillas, water & prayers, round
dance to copal, the incense that speaks into your ear, gives you inspiration,
deep inside where there is light anise. Go to Yermo's at 4:00 A.M. He'll have
the sweat lodge ready in the backyard & the sacred stones will be filling
themselves with yellow-red designs from Grandfather Fire, la luna will have
blessed you already, just smell the night perfume—that's her, covering you
with her silvery instructions. Go in now, now you are beginning, go in from
the east asking for permission to be in the circle, you ask for it by the way
you walk and move inside, it is all inside, the lodge, el fuego. Now, let the
darkness speak to the left side of you, let the smoke of sage, giving steam
waves at the center surround you, point to you, coax your beauty, hoping
for your tenderness to sing out, with your brothers & sisters, the ones you
didn't know when you entered, listen to their sighs, they are your sighs in
this one curled fragment, Little David prays out, a danzante, at the centro
cultural, a runaway, he is still searching, La Glory, who dances too, she
speaks to herself, only Grandfather Fire can circle her words, whisper
flickers, Yermo chants, eyes half-closed dreaming in, his shaky voices, pray
out, he sings, your pain, burned, the one kept to yourself, suspended, call
this out with green-deep breath into the fire stones, they are strong hearts,
they will listen, take the raw pain from your shocked nest, upheld in the
circle, give thanks, you are at the beginning, inside, empty, brilliant, leave
your harsh skin, sweat, tears, still chirping below your belly, leave them
open now where you kept them, at the center, lean with the cry, give
thanks, the fragrance is thanking you too, walk out now, silvery again,
blue-brown, out of the sacred womb-house, steam, water, earth, fire, this is
what you are, coming, going, you join the earth, go up, then, to Yermo's

after the sweat, in dance hunger, la cocina azul, get a bowl, hominy and menudo with blessings across the table, reach for the tortillas in a small basket of steam, in friendship, love, clarity & peace.

Undelivered Letters to Víctor
#7

Burciaga's death marks the end of an era, let me use these terms just once more—the end of an era. Your book marks a new one. I'll say this differently: the battles, missions, experiments, just as the feelings of chaos, frenzy, and passion continue and intersect, everything rocks on ice. Chiapas coughs up more Indian cadavers, they slide up through Perú, Oaxaca, and Guerrero— America speaks louder than our tiny books. So many Americas, that's the point: between 16th and César Chávez Boulevard, in the southern quadrant where Salvadoreños peek out of a makeshift newspaper cape on Hampshire Street cement, viejitas climb innumerable stairs into abandonment, down by the new police squad adobe on Valencia Street orange siren lights smear across store front tins and a cat with a 49er cap invites you to lean on a crucified figure, sand brown Vietnamese empanadas and an uptown Mercedes mix colors, more gold neck chain sales and steamed rice along the main line, punctuate this with cheap plastic black luggage and fried chicken, lissen to the vato preach on the corner about the coming of Quetzalcoatl II, this time the Mutton God will be dressed as a Shriner with an Uzi between his teeth firing away at McDonalds employees. South or North? Some cool guy asks as he punches out another sweet young thing, some runaway dude lost between Iowa and Canada, in between there, see?

I, Citlalli "La Loca" Cienfuegos
SUTRA ON THE NOTEBOOK

I stand alone, I hold a thousand lights in my teeth, my throat is sacred, my voice rises on its own, without the charter, only the rebel fuse, the wise elder mothers and my handsome lonely sharp-faced teen sisters, we make a fire circle, we brew the necessary liquids and nectars, topaz, obsidian, and emeraldine, reddish and deep, the caldrons are full, who can decipher us, who can locate our braids, who can truly grasp our undulating hips and fill our hearts with black sweet light, the creation spurt, this song I am singing without names and numbers and myths of time and becoming, I ask you, leaning by the armored street future? Are you ready, are you willing, are you in position or will you walk on by and carry the notebook full of nothing you know or taste or die for? The machine waits for you too, the tubing, the ancestral mezzo mump transformer interpreter translator of your self in birth form. Hear it? Can you detect its sirens? Can you alter its passage through my city, this umbral specter of sleeping moth figures.

Óyeme, Mamita
WELFARE DAYS & WELFARE NIGHTS

That should be a song for Freddy Fender, our song. All that is over too.
Tortilla Flats is out of cash for the homeless, the lonely, the lost and
abandoned sons and daughters of these ragged and misshapen streets.
Ask the governor.

Haven't forgotten him. Let me tell you. I know it is wrong to talk this way.
It really is not his fault. He's lost, punto! As Piri Thomas says. Punto, panita!
When we lived in San Diego our governor was the mayor. The poets and
artists would go up to the city administration and demand more money for
the community and he would stare at our slanted sombreros and headbands
as his face reddened a few degrees louder than our Che Guevara shirts. I
want to laugh and cry at the same time. A little cash in our tri-colored jute
bag would not have hurt, right? Of course, I am lying again. When you are
down, like we've been, money is never the answer. By the time the bills roll
in, we've transformed into being "espirituales." We've conned ourselves
into a crazier gear than the one we were living in. You know, I think I am
right, óyeme, come on. Maybe it is time to take a walk, like the old days
when we used to go to the Greyhound depot as our nightly entertainment,
watch people go places, as we sat in the wooden pews and savored our rocky
road bars. It is a deep sadness that comes to my writing friends, it rushes out
like the art they have mastered, it smolders and spits its fetus out and they
learn to recognize the torn little person, the one all poets cherish and lavish
with gifts of pain and remordimiento. We are on a dual road now. One
leads to the top, the pyramid that is, the convex-shaped tower of corporate
letters, "the system" as we used to put it, the other eggs us on, lets us slide
down the tortuous path to self-knowledge and self-immolation, it is as if
all the fiery poems, essays, stories, and novels we have written are now
running back and breaking out of their printed half-lives and are tackling
us, punishing us for giving them form and voice and exposure.

I, Citlalli "La Loca" Cienfuegos
SUTRA ON THE AUDIENCE

You must help me. I can only sing. I can only speak from this golden sea.
My feet dance on the mist, my hands high up, open and close, fold and
crest with the starry tree, la ceiba sagrada, this universe blanket I carry,
you who come, you who ride, you who crawl hunched you hitch your
revolutions, you cross from Monrovia and Kosovo, you walk barefoot and
laden with sacks of border corn from Tehuantepec, proud and ebullient,
long and short voiced, you come to me, here, you from Pristina, you from el
Norte, el Sur and you mix into my Chinatown, my Filmore, my Irish stone,
my Miwok and Castanoan catechisms, my Sausalito floors, my Sicilian caves
of desires and furies and deaths and rebirths, incandescent and gloomy and
full of solar change and solar epochs, you embroider yourselves, you paste
up your old incense and then in a minute, no, in less than a second, you
forget your eternity, your toes touching infinity, you look down at them
and you laugh, you take everything, here, everything you can from Tortilla
Flats except one thing, yourself, this you leave at the steps of the local
machine entrance way, the local mechanic displacer, time stepper, and
bender. I have no commandments, no books, no way, no rule, you must
touch, but it is not me I am really speaking of, you must swim into another
audience tonight, the audience that always speaks back, the one that hums
with every leaf and wave and wind, the wind itself, the fire itself, the waters
raging in the blue eyelash of the heavens, look up, now, you, look up, it is
all unraveling, above and below, there is nowhere to stand, nothing to say,
or write or act or be.

June Journals 6-30-88

We were living on the third floor. My dad was in the hospital with diabetes
and gangrene on his left foot. And at midnight a woman was burning alive
while everyone slept until someone knocked at our door. They screamed
Fire. I opened it. No one. Just billowing flashes and angry smoke coiling
up from the hallway. My mom who must have been about fifty-six and I
quietly stepped out the window, as if in a distant planetary spin, hushed,
our faces must have looked serenely yet gravely still like the portaits of
Vermeer or Cimabue. About 5 A.M. it was over. We stood at the bottom
entrance to the hotel with everyone else, an eerie ritual of awakening and
transition—death. My father died a year later. Everything stopped. After the
fire, I asked my mother for five dollars. Went to the movies all day. Later,
back into the woman's apartment. Looked up. Inside a shiny black violin,
its brilliant curves, its ferocious ebony, its full emptiness. How it must have
played, glowing, screaming, hot amber light, becoming white, red, black.

June Journals 6-4-88

A writer with maids. Not in my book, buddy. Never in my book. My mother was a maid in El Paso, Texas, long enough. Are writers maids, now? Who do we cook for carnal, carnala?

El Caballero invited us to an evening at the Grijalbo Awards, big publishing Shangri-la gig. And there he was, Mano Tirada. The TV, the lights, the crowd, the hors d'oeuvres, all there. There was a floating microphone going around so people could ask him things. Nobody really said nothing. Francisco asked him some high-powered five-minute Stanford question. Tirada had nothing to say. I was angry. It didn't make sense.

Writers must speak! I thought about Carlos M., another Mexicano writer that we ran into in the city, at Bellas Artes. As a matter of fact Ernesto T., a Chicano brother from Fresno was there. It was a celebration reading of another of his *Latitudes* chapbooks, *Cuentos chinos*. It was a small group reading on the outer ledge of the bookstore. Some guy asked Carlos M. what he meant by "cuentos chinos." He said it was all in the terms and that it wasn't his job to talk about it. And that was that. Arturo V., another writer there wearing overalls and long hair stumbled when I suggested that he read with music, maybe congas or any of the billion musical instruments in the Mexican cultural ecology. Even Elías Nandino gave off an odd flavor. We bumped into him on the third floor of the Torre Metropolitana where Bellas Artes runs its weekly literary rag punched together by a young crew of writers. I knew he was a bigwig from los Contemporáneos group of the forties, I knew he was gay and out with it, and he was extremely healthy, a physician and full of smiles. But that wasn't it. Somehow, it had to do with the place, his placement in a corner room on that third floor where everyone was running around as if in a shopping mall; it smelled more like an accountant's firm than a writer's turf. Somehow it had to do with the fact that everyone called him "Dr."

New York City Angelic

READING GINSBERG'S
April 16, 1997,
en route to New York

Reading Ginsberg's mid-fifties journals. Dreams, smokes, travels to Sacto, Tangiers, Paris, San José, San Francisco (Sutter & Polk corners in the rain) & the Crystal Palace view from the blue-white Greyhound on 7th—I was there. Mamá Lucha & me boppin' thru the mid-fifties. Carrying a box of lemon meringue pie to one of the tiny humid dusty theaters on Market Street to watch Manolete, the Spanish bullfighter. I open the pink carton in the back row, dip my hand into the soft sweet buttery lemon. We eat Chicano style. The bull rises. Manolete goes down in black & white sepia. Later with Rita Hayworth in *I Want to Live*. I read Ginsberg now / more so after his death. I can almost smell el tabaco después de un buen taco (Orlovsky, Burroughs, Corso—the cats in sad wrinkled suits groping for a fix on eternity, a gay immortality—beyond the flash thru the flesh—the ecstatic), as Li-Young would say, "I want to read to another audience." Recently, I was reading with my students about Huichol culture, my own trips in the '70s—to Tepic, Nayarit & the Nayar Mountains. It occurred to me that that is exactly what Huicholes do: Read to another audience. Kayaumari, Tatewarí, Tauyaupá, Nakawé, and we (although we have digital & global communication systems, institutions & trillions of "intelligence" dollars), we have no audience. Not ourselves. Not each other. Never the Multi-Eyed Spark Being of the Fire & yet we can conjure the whole, we can re-ignite our body, our soul. This very minute. This is my match. This is my kerosene. This ink lamp wicker. Illusions. The poetry biz subverts me. So.

New York City Angelic
NEED A ZEN QUOTE

Need a Zen quote. A Zen quote that will join this plane to NYC with the stalker spying on my stepdaughter, Marlene. I need a Zen quote that will loosen forty-eight years on my back, into honey braids, moss. I need a Zen quote to put into my tomato juice coming up—on ice. A quote to vibrate my thighs & bring clouds up through the jet engine. A Zen quote that doesn't need me & maybe we can strike a bargain. I need a very simple Zen quote:

> someting like:
> "Peanut bag with salt
> next to Tomato juice plastic glass
> marvelous."

I need a Zen quote that will slap my ears, say, Juan Boy! Something like this & blam! I am drinking tomatoes as I write.

Woman next to me: red-dyed hair, tattooed bracelet arms, in khakis w/ notebooks like me, splits to another seat. Cat on my right, in the middle section, headphones—probably listening to Stones or a symphony, better be listening to music instead of reports. It just occurred to me, he is listening to crap talk—he is writing! The tattoo woman writes a few rows back. The guy in front cracks a notebook-stapled report. We are all writing poetry. That's it. Poems with one hand on the chin. Poems with the left hand, clawlike, clutching the news. Poems with the mouth open for many more pretzels. Poems with the frontal image stepping & stuttering away from the mind.

New York City Angelic
PS 94

PS 94

4/17

Just hustled back from PS 94—largest elementary in Brooklyn. Between 50th & 51st. Going to be called Ezra Jack Keats Elementary but got canned because it was a Jewish name, a Jewish man—a Jew. Chicano, Latino, Puerto Rican, Central American, Dominican children: w/ big eyes & wet souls & falling back into oblivion, going back to the source without resources. Goin' to ask D.M., the vice principal how many make it out?

How many make it out, brother? Out of the tile hallways, the pasteup rooms, into full meditations, into the upward mobile soul chew ladder of apocalypse or down into the plantation brown girl brown boy Spanish-speaking tunnel. So you gotta fight like the taxi driver from Poland, five years, said you gotta make a little room, Staten Island trucking for the Mafia, the Italians, Coney Island for the Jews, Uptown for the Ricans— learn the language, he says as he crunches Polish & Americani over the cell phone to check on the limo fare as he takes me across the bridge made in 1886, he says—the year my father Felipe was born. A little history goes a long way. Five boroughs, five islands, crosshatched by misery, relocations, deportations, exiles, stories, networks, Holocaust conversations, while ordering linguini w/ shrimp & sun-dried tomatoes at Pezce Pasta on Bleeker Street—the old Dylan, Peter, Paul & Mary, Bitter End Coffee House Times Are a Changin' under-realm.

I notice our stories trading places.
We run parallel lives, someone says.
Parallels of exile
Parallels of desire boiling underwater

I listen as hard as I can. I take the bread into my right hand &
with my thumb I knife-spread the butter on, dip it into
the clear virgin oil of olives.

Óyeme, Mamita

I AM THAT PAPER

I am that paper, I am those words now, the ink burns pyres in every cell. When I look out to the trees, the long winding streets of Tortilla Flats, as they shoot to the hills and cut the electric rails of the Muni buses to the towers and Twin Peaks, the fog and into the sky haze, I see your signs, I read your voice, now I do. Yes.

Óyeme, Mamita, óyeme—now that you are gone into the deep and silent luminous fallen side of the night. Óyeme.

Papá Felipe Emilio Herrera, Wyoming, 1931

Letanía para José Antonio Burciaga

October 13, 1996,
at the old Victoria theater in San Francisco
on 16th Street where I used to
see Clavillazo & Luis Aguilar movies
while eating lobby chicharrones
in the early sixties

Ese Burciaga,
> vato de la divina tórica, vato escuadra

ruega por nosotros

ese vato muralista, con delantal de panadero,
> hacedor de pinturas y nuestras historias en paredones ilegales

ruega por nosotros

ese Tin-Tan del Chuko,

ruega por nosotros
> buzo del Segundo Barrio, Casa Zapata y de Menlo Parque

ruega por nosotros

ese poeta de la plebe bilingüe,
> escritor de milpa, misterio y esmelda

ruega por nosotros

ese tarjetero, cuate de vecindades
> en firme comunicación, cercos sueltos y campesinos en la libre

ruega por nosotros

ese vato, compañero de la Cecilia
> jefito del Toño y la Rebecca, hermano en la onda bronca

ruega por nosotros

ese cholo de Monterey
> con lápices y acrílicos y mantequilla y esperanza en la brocha

ruega por nosotros

ese Burciaga,
> tirador de botellas de colores contra los fiscales y sus changos

ruega por nosotros
ese Cantinchuko,

    de bolsa tijuanera, sacos de chiles chicanos y chistes de lobo
ruega por nosotros
ese Tony,

    profe del tomate, de la sierra en protesta y de los jarochos
ruega por nosotros
ese vato apasionado

    con letras locas, los nombres de los olvidados y

    movimientos por la justicia
ruega por nosotros
ese compa de los compas,

    con los burritos mochos y las tortillas frisbees pa' lonche
ruega por nosotros
ese silk-screen beret,

    tomando cultura y corazón en vez de Coka-Cola
ruega por nosotros
ese carnal con el fonazo político,

    con la voz urgente y las tardeadas en tu cantón al lado del 101
ruega por nosotros
ese homey del sol total,

    trozo de pan familiar y luz naciente sobre la mesa del barrio
ruega por nosotros
ese jornalero de tinta,

    voz para el pueblo, voz de oro y conciencia, voz del pobre
ruega por nosotros
ese cura con la corbata al revés

    sembrando letanías y amores, milagros sociales y flores
ruega por nosotros
ese poetazo de adobe,

    de pinole y pozole y curaciones y marchas a medianoche
ruega por nosotros
ese vatín alivianado

    de camiseta tipo camaleón, ascendente de Juariles
ruega por nosotros
ese vato machín con la guayabera tucked in,

jalando con estudiantes y hermanas carmelitas hasta el amanecer
ruega por nosotros
ese Burgie,
      armando tertulias, rondallas, barbequiadas y lunadas de hermandad
ruega por nosotros
ese Tony con Tony Lamas del Río Grande
      en el Bracero Bar, en Madera Roja, dibujando las verdades
ruega por nosotros
ese jacalero de mi cora, cantando
      "San Antonio" en vez de Santone,
      "El Paso del Norte" en vez de El Pasowe
Sabes qué, carnal José Antonio, la verdad es que
      me canso
      me canso de no verte
         me canso de no escucharte
      de no sentir tu ternura a mi lado
      pero yo te recuerdo
      y no me olvido, la verdad es que
      no sé más que no olvidarte
      no sé más que siempre escucharte
            en esta vereda aquí

ese Burciaga, ese padrino del divino bolo, ese alacrán buti suave
      aquí te cantamos, en caló, en calor y puro amor.
Amén, Awimin
y Con Safos.

On the Other Side of Puccini's

(NORTH BEACH, SAN FRANCISCO, 1994)

for my brother, Jim Sagel,
who went out too fast.
Gracias for the chicos &
the sopaipillas de Española,
for the all voices
you found
nesting beneath
the broken stones.
4/23/98

Spark the red lowriders of Española, at the bottom rung of la estafeta
where Don Apolonio reads mail from R. T. Jameson's real estate company
in Kingman, Arizona, says he's gonna get "unos acres pa' mijo." Just thirty
dollars a month. But soon he's going to die from diabetes and the money,
well, you know. And on the way home, his tiny wife, La Luchita, advises,
"Mire, ya no coma esas costillas, puro sebo, le hace mal." Don Apolonio
quips in his usual fast beat: "Mírame bien, ves aquí," he slides his finger
down his neck and plucks his Adam's apple, "A mí me gusta que me escurra
el sebo hasta el gaznate." A few miles up the hill in Llano, Don Fresca asks
Cavallari for help, el Argentino who's been up in these parts for years with
his little daughter Mielita, days since the hippies rolled into town. But first,
before you bale the hay, lemme see your hands . . . pa' ver si sabes trabajar.
Old man Fresca barks out, "¡Tienes manos de masa! What do you do?"
I write, I tell him. I smash landscapes together. My father died of diabetes
not Apolonio. It was me who drove into Taos in search of the gods in '74.
I met Sagel in Española in '84, with my lover Margarita, la de los ojos de
bruja. We stepped into Teresa's and Jim's adobe. Hecho a mano, says Jim.
I'll show you how if you like. But first, here, have some chicos con chile,
unas sopaipillas. We go for a walk outside. Take some baling wire, Jim says
in his ruffled smooth voice as he picks up the dark jagged spiral from the
flat dirt. For the hard times. Suave, I say with my San Francisco–El Paso
twang. El Jim sits back in the porche on a tiny wooden chair as we leave.
Winds curl the winter leaves. The afternoon blurs into a coppery wave.
Maybe, you'll sell me cinco acres, I ask him before I open the rented car.

Yeah, pones tu traila allí en frente and we'll talk in la resolana. That's it. We laugh out loud, then look away. Years go by in Iowa, then back to Fresno. We're talking about all this on Columbus Street, San Francisco, nine something P.M., after Jim's poetry reading in the Mission District. We're across the street from Puccini's having a Thai peanut butter pizza, medium size. Jim smiles at me. I mumble and stretch to one side. Sirens and hipsters shoot by the neon-spoked dreamy night. How about a smoke? I ask. Tienes el Velvete? Lo tengo. Y el baling wire que te di en Española? He asks me. Balances the hand-rolled bacha between his thin fingers. Jim is about to say a few more words as the sharp flame lights up his kind still face.

Conmigo no se juega.—Popular saying

Mamá Lucha and Juanito
at the Greyhound photo booth,
San Diego, California, 1960

HISPAVISION PRESENTS

Hispanopoly

THE UPWARDLY MOBILE IDENTITY GAME SHOW

VOICES

ANNOUNCER: Mod, upbeat, snazzy

SANCHO ON SUNDAY: Stereotypical sellout

WANNA B. WHITE: Throaty voice

LA MIGRA: Southern twang

CONTESTANTS #1, #2, #3: Innocent stand-bys

AUDIENCE: Into it

SET

A TV game show (a mix of *Jeopardy* and *Wheel of Fortune,* somewhere in the Post-Macho Southwest, slouching through the twenty-first century).

SOUND DESIGN

Audience cilantro ambiance in background.

ANNOUNCER: [*champagne music / a la Laurencio Welk, voice over*]
Hispanopoly is sponsored by TAA, Tan American Airlines [*sound of jet*] "Where your fly is always open." [*echo effect*] And M.A.C.Y.S. "Mexican American Contras Yearning for Cash." [*sound of machine guns and then coins pouring into a bucket*] And now, our game show host, the renown Hispanologist, Dr. Eso Es, Sancho On Sunday [*drum roll with charro grito*], the inventor of the first Coyote Hisputnik across Tijuana! [*sound of rocket ship engines*] Heeeeeeeeeere's Sancho!

[*tortilla chip crunch sounds, then applause*]

SANCHO: Órale, meh yamoh Sancho on Sunday. Bean venidos to the only game where your color is really a tan. As you know, our game assistant

Wanna B. White [*applause*] will spin the upwardly mobile wheel for you and read you the Hispa-trend. Ready, Wanna?

WANNA B.: ¿Qué? ¿Qué? Shoe wanna what? [*canned laughter*] Jalapeños score ten points, tamales, twenty, and organic carrot enchiladas, fifty.

[*applause*]

SANCHO: Today our top prizes are—

WANNA B.: A 2003 two-tone Chevy-con-Bush Slowrider.

[*sputtering, pop*]

SANCHO: The only car in America where the engine runs on Dos Okies. [*charro grito, applause*] And one hundred pesos of Hillary Bonds so you can turn your peso into a big pedo. [*train steam, canned laughter*] Wanna, what else?

WANNA B.: A grand prize of one hundred kilos of PRI cigars made of the finest blend of Zapatista tobacco leaves and a round trip for two to the Mayan rain forest in Chiapas—where you'll stay at the luxurious PEMEX (Please Exit Mildly Except for Xenophobics) Motel.

[*machine guns and monsoon rain sounds*]

SANCHO: Órale. Contestants remember to crunch your microwave hard-shell tortillas when you think you have an answer to the Hispa-clue. [*crunch*] Órale. The first category is "Financial Management."

[*charro grito*]

WANNA B.: ¿Qué? ¿Qué?

[*canned laughter*]

SANCHO: Oh, yes, contestants remember a Chicano is not a Hispanic. Wanna B., spin me! [*firecrackers, wheel spin that slows down*] Wanna, read the card please.

[*charro grito*]

WANNA B.: "How to use your Fruit-of-the-Loom T-shirt to divert attention from your bad credit."

SANCHO: Contestant número uno?

CONTESTANT #1: [*crunch sounds*] Hispa-chute! [*applause*] "Sports" for two hundred, por favor.

[*applause*]

WANNA B.: [*firecrackers, wheel spin*] "A martial art technique that numbs your opponent's sense of color awareness."

[*canned laughter*]

CONTESTANT #1: [*crunch sounds*] Hispa-ratee! [*applause*] "Wines" for three hundred, por favor.

[*applause, firecrackers, wheel spin*]

WANNA B.: "Light wine bouquet casually wrapped around you during an interview about your wetback past."

[*canned laughter*]

CONTESTANT #1: Uhh. híjolas, nel, no me la sé—chihuahua—

[*siren, muffled sounds, car door opens, walkie talkie, fast footsteps, enter LA MIGRA*]

LA MIGRA: [*enters through tortilla curtain*] Excuse me, seenyor, ID please, passport. Howdy, Sancho, nice fiesta here, this will take just uno minutoh.

[*applause, handcuffs, screams, curtain closes, sirens, car drives away*]

SANCHO: He was showing signs of weakness. [*baby gurgling*] Contestant number two step up please. Órale. [*canned laughter*] Can you repeat that, Wanna?

[*crunch*]

WANNA B.: "Light wine bouquet casually wrapped around you during an interview about your wetback past."

[*applause*]

CONTESTANT #2: [*crunch*] What is Hispa-blush! [*applause, charro grito*] "Jogging" for one hundred please.

WANNA B.: [*wheel spin*] "Flat style of pacing yourself so as not to appear gay in an after–Cinco de Mayo macho-disco dance."

CONTESTANT #2: Uhh—

[*crunch*]

SANCHO: Contestant number two, spik up, por favor.

CONTESTANT #2: What is the Hispa-stroll! [*charro grito, applause*] "Cuisine" for three hundred, por favor.

[*applause*]

WANNA B.: [*firecrackers, wheel spin*] The next Hispa-clue is "Low cholesterol, chili-shaped, intentionally bland, mango-flavored Chapstick for the Hispa-loid on the run (can be ordered in various colors)."

[*canned laughter*]

CONTESTANT #2: [*crunch*] What is a Hispa-stick! [*applause, charro grito*] "Automobiles" for one hundred please.

WANNA B.: [*wheel spin*] Listen carefully: "New cockroach gas-filler substitute developed by Hispanics for the Non-Union Agribusiness Committee."

[*canned laughter*]

CONTESTANT #2: [*crunch*] Uhh—Hispa—uhhhhh. Híjola, I mean—Hispa—

[*sirens, muffled sounds, door opens, walkie talkie, enter* LA MIGRA]

LA MIGRA: Passport, por favor. Howdy, Sancho, we got us another Bean Venido!

[*sirens, screams, fade*]

WANNA B.: What is "Hispa—zoil," pendejo! Phew!

[*applause*]

SANCHO: Our time is almost up. Órale, contestant number three, trucha.

[*charro grito*]

CONTESTANT #3: "Modern Art" for three hundred, por favor.

[*applause*]

WANNA B.: [*firecrackers, wheel spin*] "The art of taking your manager's decor ideas to your house so you can escalate your status on the day she or he comes over to taste your version of carne asada."

[*canned laughter*]

CONTESTANT #3: Yayah! [*crunch, crunch*] What is His-Picasso! [*applause*] "Politics" for fifty please.

WANNA B.: [*firecrackers, wheel spin*] Here we go: "A self-taught Republican correspondence course for correcting over-reaching tongue action in the face of capital gains."

CONTESTANT #3: [*crunch*] What is Hispa-my-lips!

[*applause*]

SANCHO: Órale. Now we have the Hispa-championship. Are you ready contestant number three? Hold on to your cilantro green ID card. Wanna, please read the category.

[*applause*]

WANNA B.: [*crunch, charro grito*] The last catagory is—"Upwardly Mobile Beverages."

[*foaming beverage pouring sound*]

AUDIENCE: Oooooooohhhhh!

WANNA B.: [*crunch, wheel spin*] Listen up, pendejo! "The beverage you carry to your Minority Affairs lecture that will help you look bilingual."

CONTESTANT #3: [*crunch*] Hispa—

SANCHO: Contestant number three? [*heart throb sound*] Are you there?

CONTESTANT #3: [*crunch, crunch, crunch, crunch*] Hispa—Peppy? Hispa—Pepsi?

[*gong, enter* LA MIGRA, *handcuffs, screams, walkie talkie, car driving off, screams, canned laughter, applause*]

SANCHO: Órale. Congratulations, mocoso. [*charro grito*] Here are your tickets to the jungle. [*charro grito*] Say hello to Gortari on the way through Kazakhstan. Enjoy the ride on Tan American Airlines "where your fly is always open." [*echo*] And Wanna B., what Hispa-trend clue do we have for our suburban participants?

WANNA B.: "Mucho Fashion," Sancho. Please identify the following new fashion trend, pendejos: "Beef-flavored non-cholesterol polyester campesino-print handkerchief, also comes in plaid pork and two-tone menudo."

SANCHO: Please send in your answers on the back of a Taco Smell wrapper. ¡Órale, que vivan los Sanchos!

[*applause*]

WANNA B.: [*champagne music*] ¿Qué? ¿Qué? What?

ANNOUNCER: [*crunch, crunch*] Órale. [*re-wind, champagne music, voice over*] This is *Hispanopoly*, your upwardly mobile life game [*jet engine sound*] that promises you to gain your true identity through the acquisition of someone else's property, usually lower than you [*canned laughter*]—your live-in Indian maid from Latin America that's running away from genocide, for example. [*machine guns and rain, applause, charro grito, cut off by static*] Stay tuned for more.

SANCHO: Hey, the migra took the Chevy!

[*squealing tires, crashing sounds, broken glass*]

AUDIENCE: Oooooohhhhhhhhhhh. ¡Ajua!

[*crunch, crunch*]

ANNOUNCER: All prizes are sponsered by MIGRA-187-209-277 Studios.
(Mucho Interesante Grab-You Right Away, Inc.)

Ever Split Your Pantalones
While Trying to Look Chingón?

For all hard-core Chicano lawyers who have never
admitted to anyone that they
are ex-altar boys

Like when I was coming back from a Santana Blues Band Concert at the
Filmore, back in '67—this guy with a Led Zeppelin black leather jacket laid
a pastrami & mota barf on my back, like, like when I was serving misa de
gallo at our Lady of Guadalupe on Kearny Street, in '61 and Padrecito
Benjamín was raising the Host for benediction ("Watch his hands," they
told me) and I had to ring the bell with my right hand just like the altar boy
champion José Rendieta, but I was left-handed so I rang it with my right
hand and it sounded like guacamole, like, like when I first met Margie, took
her to the Hungry Tiger in North Beach and we danced, had Cannelloni,
came back to visit my buddies Demarest and Álvarez and Eva L. (Demarest's
novia) who made tons of pilipino refín and wanting to impress Eva &
Margie, I wolfed the pancit, washed it down with smokes & two tall glasses
of rum that I thought were Coca-Cola and barfed on the red carpet with
music note designs on them as I broke over the leather armchair like that, or
like in '58 when we went to Tijuana & I was wearing the wool, Mexicano
double-breasted suit that my tío Fernando wanted me to wear to the cine
Bujazán to watch *La momia azteca* until I was sweating so hard that when
I touched the metal seat in front of me during a María Félix kiss, I electro-
cuted myself, screamed so loud they turned the houselights on, everyone
thought I was dying, like this, like when I burned my mustache off trying to
blow out my birthday kequi or like when I stood up at St. Anthony's and my
pantalones had eaten themselves into my cuchi-cuchi and everyone in the
back rows, especially Doña Aguado, La Católica, looked at it. Like that.

Two Tacos al Pastoral

I. How to Comb Your Hair High Up Like a Tipi

Albina closed her eyes
as she stepped into a hot eucalyptus bath. You were there too, in that old
adobe mobile home, just a few miles north of Santa Fe. Except you always
deny it.

You were the one that complained about Garibaldi, our stray tomcat that
managed to scratch through the baked adobe axles and make two donut-
shaped holes into the kitchen so he could get at some of the three hundred
honey-coated buñuelos that Grandma Sofía stacked on the table. You
haven't forgotten have you? Why don't you remember? You were the one
who slipped half a can of Crisco shortening into the tub, probably just to
see what would happen to our older sister, Albina.

You knew it was her quinceañera. Albina was having a coming-out party
and you said she was stealing away all your friends. I don't know, but I saw
you hiding behind the adobe ice box, near the front door. When Albina
came out into the yard, it started to happen. Slowly, her long braided hair
began to sponge up to the sky, as she approached our father, all dressed up
for the first time—he even said he felt like "un pingüino americano," and
our dear mother with a pound of black rosaries around her neck. Later you
asked Mom if her rosaries were made out of chocolate "cause she always
smelled them before she put them over her head." You must remember.

Mom heard you laugh out loud and scream. We all did. Padre Rasura blessed
fifteen-year-old Albina when little Jesús Aguacate, her escort, opened his
mouth and couldn't stop. Father Rasura thought little Jesús had suddenly
been possessed by the diablo. So he threw little Jesús down on the dirt and
pounded on his chest with the bible and asked Abuelita Sofía to stuff him

with all the buñuelos she could carry because "the devil doesn't like burnt sweet breads." And Albina? Wait. I must confess. Jesús wasn't an aguacate, I just called him that. One day I gave him a flat top with Dad's barbershop cutter and discovered that his skull was the exact shape of an avocado; from that day on I called him "Aguacatito." What was his last name?

Albina just stood there in her starched and pleated pink French thing we bought in downtown Santa Fe. She knew something had happened to her. She said "there is something very heavy above me, maybe it's a sign from heaven." You were screaming in tears. After Little Jesús had been smothered with buñuelos and his clothes were so sticky he barely could walk to the well to wash up, that's when mom fell to her knees. Mamá touched Albina's hair and crossed herself. Her braids had sprung up about ten feet and fanned out into a thick and crazy butterfly with red ribbons for antennas. You must remember, it wasn't that long ago we stopped cooking with Crisco.

II. My Chickens Say, "Por favor, sí señor, sí señora"

Of course chickens don't talk—this was the first piece of common knowledge that had to be discarded. When Antoinne Saldívar Exclamado came back from Stanford, after a four-year stint for a B.A. in economics, the first thing he did was set the record straight for the rest of his familia.

The Exclamados lived in West Liberty, sixteen miles south of Iowa City, Iowa. The poultry business was in their blood, or should I say on their clothes? Exclamado Sr. had managed to start up a two-truck turkey transport enterprise that would haul the feathery toms from the ranches near Muscatine and Conesville to the Iowa Beef plant in West Liberty. From there, they would be sorted out in the shape of approximately seventy-six processed meat products. They were scientific agents and nutrients in the form of bacon, weenies, fry-strips, colored gel, ligament particle hams, four calorie levels of bologna, and naturally as water-based Thanksgiving-groomed, air-proof plastic packs en route to all points east and west. Exclamado Jr. had a plan to expand the ma & pa makeshift business into a corporate bird giant: Tom Exclamado Central, Inc.

Antoinne was busy drafting the papers and blueprints. Young Exclamado sketched feverishly into the night for weeks upon his return to his hometown. He drew up ideas for "Turbert," a turkey bologna sherbert, "Sharkies," a new fish and chicken meat cracker for preschoolers and the college generation, "Turk-Bees," hand-size tortilla-shaped poultry-flavored jerky chews. Most of all, he was polishing designs for "Tommy-Disc," a turkey ligament-based software disc. You could use it to store computer information and when out of use, you could eat it with a thin spread of Turbert. One glitch he had to work on was the "Burp Virus" that emanated fowl odors from the monitor. Junior kept on. "Feed your screen, feed your brain," this was the motto Exclamado had carved on his desk while at Stanford.

Things developed quickly for the Exclamados. A rocket lab in Vladivostok, Russia, wanted "Tommy-Disc" for biodegradable satellites; in Hollywood, Wisney Studios started a cartoon series, "The Adventures of Tommy-Disc in Cyberspace." In Europe, "Le Turbert Swing," a new music and dance craze, swept across the landscape into Norway. Girls in Rome wore a corn-based edible one-piece round flannel cloth tied over their shoulders and were called "Turbertinas." In a few short whiffs, Tom Exclamado Central Inc. became a global phenomenon.

Fidencia Exclamado, Antoinne's mamá, was the only one to notice a drawback. She carried a tiny greenish notebook where she jotted "La habladera," a strange set of vowel sounds that Exclamado Jr. had developed since his return to the old two-truck business. At night when everyone was asleep in the new blue house, purchased with "Tom" profits and when all the animals were in the roost, you could hear Antoinne's peculiar snoring. A chicken squawk and turkey bleat opera, the new melody from the young accountant's mouth. If you perched yourself next to his Turbert notebooks, you could see him jerking his head to one side, then to the other. If you stayed long enough, until the break of day, you could follow him to the corrals, where he crawled, flapped his elbows, and joined up with the sundry squad of hens and raven-colored roosters in saluting the new sun.

Three Surefire Ethnic Sitcoms

I. The Lost Picasso Enchilada Silhouettes: A "Noba Yor" Story

When Picasso arrived in Noba Yor (he pronounced New York this way being that he was searching for his Mexican Roots), he sported a gabardine ruffled trench coat—printed with the image of Jimi Hendrix melting his guitar with cigarette lighter fluid, a chartreuse Day-Glo silk screen; cool trick he had learned early on in Paris, Texas, with his buddy Juan Grifo.

It was a Friday, the best day for any Spaniard ready to blow the week through a tiny shot of anís and a blackish dunce cone of hard bread. It was Friday and Picasso sat at the Cilantro Café bar.

The Cilantro used to be the Limbo Shirt Shop in the East Village but that was all over now. "The limbo is in the cilantro," this he had heard from Juan Grifo. "The limbo is in the cilantro," he said to himself as he tossed another shot of clear hot syrup down the hatch and mumbled something to the waitress, Hanoi, a muscular Puerto Rican Vietnamese woman who was known for her knowledge of Mexican wrestling history.

"Look, Hanoi, I jes gots to los New Yorrrrks, you know what I means, rrrrright?

"No."

So he mumbled a bit louder. This Picasso guy with the funny coat and the blue velvet beret was a weirdo at the old Limbo Cilantro. But Hanoi was drawn to him. "If only he wouldn't roll his *R*'s so hard," she mumbled to herself. "If only he'd drop the phony accent and the lousy talk."

"Why's everboda mumbling aroun' here, anyways," Picasso said out loud. "I jes wanna know about one ting."

Some wrinkled guy with white corduroy loafers barked back from a small wedge table parked in the middle of the video game machines. He was munching on a dry chunk of sweet potato pie from the Automat. "What 'ting' are you referring to?"

"Why don't you mind your own frijoles, besides you owe me a game from last night," Hanoi shouted as she turned to Picasso.

"What 'ting'? The art 'ting'?" she asked.

Hanoi swished her complex pompadour toward the short, plump guy with the blue beret and polka-dot vest. Her greenish eyes locked into him.

"What 'ting' are you interested in Sam?"

"Les put it dis way." Picasso unzipped his pants and pulled out an old orange-colored tamale leaf from his hidden eel skin wallet.

"See this? See wha's written on this tamale leaf? You don't see it, do you? You don't see what I've been carrying. You tink dis is easy, sweetie? Ever since I was in Paris I've been hauling this thin baby around. I could be in a tough straights, I could be in the good times, but I always gots this one on me. My great-granpapi gave it to my granpapito and he gave it to my papi. My pops snuck it across the Pyrenees wrapped into a knot under his right arm pits for months, he called it 'el sobaquito,' then my mamá carried it rolled into a dough ball strung aroun' her 'stómago. See? She told the border guards it was a baby. 'Es una papa sin papers, please let him cross.' She named her Tomasita. We called her Masita for shortnin', little dough ball, get it? Anyway we had to leave 'cuz we didn't have a green card for La Masita."

Hanoi listened hard, squeezed a muscle ball with her left hand.

"After couplah of years blam! The people from the village were wonerin' what was going on. Mamá told 'em that Tomasita was a curse from God. 'La cursera,' she sang, wit her hands up in the air like she was playing the tambourine, you know, She said a revelación from the Madonna of Toledo came down one night while she was makin' chicken mole for dinner. 'The Madonna told me that I have to carry Tomasa thrice as long as other women cause when I was a girl I had desired too many tings—especially Mr. Garcilaso's tomatoes, you know, the TV Latino "three-minute salsa" gourmet—right?'"

Hanoi popped the muscle ball with her curved black fingernails. The sand spilled into her lemonade and onto the sleek table. "I said I am listening, OK?" She said as she puckered her burgundy-painted lips and blew the sand over the top.

"The Madonna also said that Tomasa needed 'un picaso' to be born: a pinch, a prick, a tiny hole so she could burst forth. Three years later, blam, I was there. My mamá raised her hands up again and before we knew it, we were hanging out in East Los Angeles. We were dressed up like comedians. I played Harpo González and screwed up my face—you see I couldn't tolk English, my little brother Fidel was Groucho, but instead of a cigar he sucked on a green onion. Papi was Ricky Rockardo and Mamá was La Lucy."

"You were Harpo? Come on. Harpo Rockardo?"

"I was crunchin' my face and playing a fake saxophone, like the presidente and blam out rolled La Tomasa—the dough ball, from under Mamá's American flag shawl on Olvera Street, you know that place where all the tourists come to see the minorities do their how-to-make-a-tortilla ting?"

"You mean Olvera Street in the middle of the plaza where they throw quarters to the people and pieces of burgers to the pigeons?" Hanoi grunted as she curled a large jar of jalapeños with her right arm.

"Yeah, right, anyway, blam, in the middle of that old crusty dough ball was this tamale leaf. And in the center of this leaf there was this address: 1436 North. The Cilantro Café! See whadday mean? Blam!"

"But why here?" Hanoi asked, rolling up her sleeves, showing Picasso the face of La Santa Filomena, the famous female masked Mexican wrestler from Guanajuato etched in blue black jail needle ink on her left bicep.

"The enchildada silhouettes . . ." Picasso replied in a low voice.

"What?"

"You know what I said . . . enchiladas. Thass what this is all abou', alright?"

Hanoi knew what he was talking about. She knew it. She relaxed her thick left arm, took a breath, and called the dude with the white corduroy loafers.

"Hey, Colorado, come here, please. There's a job for you to do. Please retrieve the enchilada silhouettes from the basement, you know what I am alluding to? Of course you do. Remember the salsa party we threw years ago?"

"Tree years to be sakly." Colorado called back from the Space Rangers machine. His face was glowing neon sparkles as he rolled the power ball. He had just hit a big score and was feeling good.

"Well, Sam, here is looking for some of the plates that were left, you recollect how everybody was talking about it, right?"

Colorado shuffled up to Picasso and Hanoi, shaking his little head from one side to the other, singing a tune to himself. Whistling.

"Yeah, I remembah. Sally tree fingers was out that day, she usually made the gourmet stuff when we trew a party. So's her sister, La Bruja from Brooklyn, made the enchiladas that morning. And 'cuz she had a beef wit me for going out wit La Rosa from Queens, she put a spell on the salsa. I remembah.

Everybody was hallucinating. Especially the guys that tote they were bettah than us, you know those Hispanic types that come 'round heah in their tree-piece suits and rebuilt El Dorados and '81 Celicas."

"That's right," Hanoi chimed in, "last year you set fire to Octaviano's dusty Camero on Cinco de Mayo, the guy that bought out Rico & Luigi's Italian Colombian sausage deli down the block. Yeah, those new Hispanic types got it worse than anybody else. They went over the verge, they began to see shadows following them wherever they went. Bean-shaped shadows, dark brown puddles behind 'em—in front too."

"Everwheah." Colorado was nervous and giggling. "You really want me to go down and get the platos?"

"Get off your behind and bring 'em up to me, 'cause I think we have some business with Mr. New Yorks. OK?" Hanoi said tightening her hair, leaning at the bar, giving Picassito the look.

"All I want to do is take some pictures. Maybe the silhouettes have someting to do wit me and my familia, wit all of us. México. América—wit Hollywood."

Hanoi nodded her head, said "Hollywood" and gulped another fast drink of spearmint and lemonade, one of the Cilantro specials. Picasso and El Colorado rushed down the stairs near the freezers, all the way until they came upon a red Samsonite suitcase at the bottom step.

"Thass were we put 'em in, in there; the enchiladas were spreading out, sprouting little pineapple heads, so's we locked them up. Kinda looks sporty, right?" Before Picasso could answer, El Colorado turned around and left him alone.

Picasso stared. Kneeled down before the red suitcase. He lifted his hands up like his mamá and prayed out loud to La Madonna of Toledo, the one that El Greco the great Spanish painter had seen in a stormy vision that caused him to paint madly until his death. Little Picasso thought of the stretched faces and torsos that El Greco painted after his vision. He thought of his mamá back in East Los Angeles waiting for him, boiling a chicken, plucking out the feathers, her eyes rolling around the room ready for a sign from above, waiting for another leaf or even a floating piece of chorizo from the heavens. Maybe the tamale leaf would lead him to riches like the Hispanic types, maybe it was a message for a revolution on Olvera Street? Or was it simply a better recipe for salsa de tomate. Just maybe it spelled out the secreto to his own tiny mixed up Spanish Mexican soul, the little voice that always tickled him and urged him to paint triangle female faces and trapezoid hips on men. Picassito crossed himself with the tamale leaf and opened the bright Samsonite luggage piece.

"Hey Sam, ¿qué pasó?" Hanoi yelled from above. "Did you hit the restroom or something? What do you take me for? Do I resemble some kind of goofy Pocahontas waiting for your flat behind?"

"Wait a minuto, OK?"

"Five minutes, we close, brotherito. So get your tortillas together."

"Yeah, yeah," he said as he opened the suitcase. For a while he let the ruby light bathe him. His face changed. His fake accent transformed. A deep breath lifted every delicate bone in his body. After he closed the case, he was never the same. He went off with Hanoi to Paris, Texas. Picasso's mamá moved in and opened up a restaurant and wrestling business called La Virgen de Toledo Federation. Colorado was the headwaiter and MC who also checked out towels. Soon Colorado started a wrestling designer towel enterprise called Tú Allá, Inc. At the Cilantro Café, they still laugh about the day Picasso walked in with his tight trench coat.

Near the windows of La Virgen de Toledo Federation, next to the shrine for the Madonna, there is a Jimi Hendrix video game machine that spins out rock tunes every time you hit over a thousand. The whole place lights up in Day-Glo green paisley notes and everybody sings "Foxy Lady" in Spanish

("Lobita mía"). Picasso walks around with a dough ball wrapped around his "'stómago," says it is the only way to keep in touch with his sister, La Tomasita. Hanoi framed the enchilada silhouettes, became a curator, and opened up the "Harpo González Galería" next to the kitchen. It reads "Welcome to Noba Yor."

II. Juantoomany

Say, hullo there.

Forget it.

I say hello but no one listens except myself and you, of course. Maybe it's my crazy two-tone Armani dance shoes, the fuchsia tights. Or maybe I just had Juantoomanys. Everywhere I look there is a Juan. Can't help it. It's true. Can't knock it, can't shake it. Everywhere I turn there's a Juan. Just yesterday I rolled out a dollar bill at the local liquor shop. You know, I was playing Lotto and maybe I was thinking things would change a little. But the machine spit the peso out like a little backward tortilla roller. That's when I noticed the tiny mustache on George. He doesn't have one, right? Ever seen a mustache on good ol' George Washington? Never. But, gees, there it was as clear as guacamole on a Macy's shirt. George Juanshington. My pockets were full of 'em too. A pocket full of Juans. Juans and Georges. Which is who? I get 'em mixed up. That's why you don't see me at parties anymore. The nervous tick gets the best of me. My neck pops back twice, in a funny syncopated mambo beat. It usually happens when I hear someone talking in Español. You see, I don't do Español either. I use to do Español, but it got me in a lot of trouble. How would you like to go around waving your hands up and down, arching your eyebrows, explaining why your house isn't in the shape of a pyramid? That's how I met my wife, Margajuana, actually. She was the only other expert on pre-Columbian Mayan temple architecture in Pennsylvania. But she left me. Said that I had my Classic Guatemala in the wrong place or was it the wrong period? Anyway that's why I'm here, lying down on your Naugahyde. Don't feel sorry, I get around pretty good. Juanever I want to, I pop in a video. My favorite Juan is *Juan Flew Over the Cuckoo's Nest*. Do you identify with Jack Nicholsjuan? Sure is hard not to. The movie reminds me of my dream to return to Argentina one day. Just wait and see; me in a tango and a violin, a presidential affair, a pink tux, brilliant spats. Margajuana sips from an oval maté cup with a fancy tin straw and a little wiry beaker at the end to keep out the straw. I'll be the rage in a blue beanie like Jack, just Juanderful. What? You're right. There I go again. Easy as Juan, two, three. Can't shake it. Can't knock it. Take up Italian, that's what my wife used to say. Learn a little about Giotto and Micheljuangelo. Ancient marble carved into microscopic dancers with fat bellies. Culture's good for you, expand, she said. Feed on Florentine and Tuscan almonds, a sip of Chianti. Taste another sandwich of language. You'll see how everything will change. Effortless. Couldn't buy the tickets, though. Living in a Juandominium was expensive. So, I stayed in Philly, scribbled on napkins. Sculpted Mohammed Alis and Davids on Ivory soap. For a while, my Juana Lisas on paper towels were a hit at the Greyhound stations. Things began to get smooth, I moved to San Francisco, worked on the wharf. Ate crab and chop suey for years and drew cartoons for the tourists. Until this morning. I told you already didn't I? Got busted for selling T-shirts without a permit. Swear they were a hit: "Welcome to the Juanited States of America." What's wrong with a Juan—Juans in a while? I don't do dots or spots. You're never going to catch me doing spots. Lines? Do I look like someone that does lines? Look at me: Max J. Gomesindo Jr., cartoonist, Italian art historian, connoisseur of Olmec and Mayan archeology. My father, Max Juanete, did have the mambo tick, now that I remember. Five or six years old, I was just a baby; saw him twist into a mambo spasm when my mother, Rufina, explained the meaning of the universe to him. She quoted Einstein's theory of relativity as she held her right hip with one hand, danced across the trailer floor and with the free hand she spun a large flour tortilla over my head. She sang out in a throaty voice—"Listen to me, Max, you really want to know why we are here in San Juan Capistrano and not back there in Juanos Aires? I'll tell you. It's like Don Alberto says, OK? Light travels at the speed of Juan. Here today, Juan tomorrow."

III. La Llorona Power-Woman Confidential

Classified Sheet: La Llorona Meets Dr. Espanto

Des E. Torny-Yadda is one of her secret identities: a short, dark brunette with thick glasses, a mole on her left cheek and a knock-kneed gait. Family from East Juárez, Chihuahua. Jumped the border illegally and took up residence in El Paso, Texas. Graduated from Jefferson High and went on to UCLA; paid her way by selling Mayan herbal hangover lotions to the Greek frats by Hedrick Hall.

Des E. is a human mask, a useful day-to-day moniker in the big city haze of mauve-colored offices, stiletto acquaintances, and smog-squeezed personas. On a clear day you can flip your head back, gaze up, and count most of the thirty stories of the Barrel Linch TransAmerican Tower in the financial district of San Francisco. She now works as a broker on floor 27: International Investments. Her male Latino colleagues call her *desatornillada,* "screwy, crazy sellout" or Des for short. Envy, cold stares and menudo-smelling blazers do not phase DTY. Old macho dogs caught in a downward career spiral, these she gobbles with a Granola bar and washes them down with a half cup of 2% fat milk as she downloads trade data from ITT and Microsoft.

"TY" is what her white coworkers call her when they see her stepping out to a Coho Salmon Cappuccino brunch with Dr. Espanto Esparza, the highest paid VP in the business.

"TY's got what it takes—brains, brains, and more brains," they say biting their glossy fingernails, praying for a break.

What the junior brokers don't know is that by night TY takes on another ID. She presses the computer code at the gray marble entrance door in the private parking lot, slides up the elevator, and swishes back into Espanto's terminal where she swims through the global files of Barrel Linch, milking accounts in Switzerland into guerrilla files on the Nicaraguan coast, undoing New York diamond notes and dropping them into the Underground Indian and Peasant Front on the border between Chiapas and Yucatán.

They call her "La Llorona" because, as the Indians say, "she has come back to save her children." In fact, "La Llorona" is her code name on the Internet; she appears and disappears in a keystroke. Bank of America, Banco Serfín, Banamex, Sumitomo, Maritime Arctic Bank of Commerce; they have all been gauged and bitten by the shadowy electric hand of "La Llorona." It is reported that Des E.'s current project is to hit W.H.A.T., otherwise known as W. Hey All Houser Timber, Incorporated, in Seattle. A note was found in their quarterly Board of Directors agenda: "Eliminate environmental disaster, save the spotted owls and the last great redwoods or I'll bite your heads off!"

Today Dr. Espanto noticed that his Van Gogh screen saver was jittery, the mouse pad upside down—there definitely was something wrong. His Virgen de Guadalupe frame was turned backward. Espanto's family album of three, Shannon, his wife, Erin, and Espantito, the cross-eyed baby, was crooked as if someone had pulled the photos and then replaced them in a hurry. Breathing hard, he turned to get a cup of caffeine from his espresso machine and saw the brief letter, a print-out, addressed to him:

Dr. Espanto:
You've got exactly seven hours and seven minutes to change the fate of the world. And I am going to see that Destiny moves kindly. First of all, you must do the following (or boo-hoo: you may watch your family fotos on the next *America's Most Wanted* TV show, brought to you by the FBI computer files):

uno: Deposit all the Washington, DC, presidential lobby accounts into the #12 Vata-Chiapas file;

dos: Pentagon and NASA budget investments in earthmovers, hydro-electric power loans, and environmental clean-up accounts move to #441 Chava-Rwanda account;

tres: Promote all the women on your staff, immediately, or I'll bite your head off!

La Llorona

Dr. Espanto filled his Vesuvio cup with a double espresso, sat down, and stared into a Chinatown shrunken into a tiny green square down below. He took a bite from an old custard empanada pastry his mother had left him four months ago, on Father's Day. A funny taste radiated through his mouth, a musky air came up to his nostrils. As he crouched over his monitor and followed "La Llorona's" instructions, he sniffed again. The perfume was familiar. "Des E. Torny-Yadda wears this brand, Z-Lantro—a fancy new rain forest musk made out of tropical grasses," Espanto whispered as he deleted the transactions. He would wait for the night; Dr. Espanto screwed his eyes. In a New Age mask, one of those gray clear gels—with a red bandanna and a black hat, he would peer behind his office door. Things were about to change fast. "Just wait, baby," he laughed to himself with a new air of confidence, "tomorrow, in the *Daily Salsa Examiner,* in bold letters, the headline is gonna read: Mystery Masked Man Saves Nation. Latina Culprit Captured by Exec!"

To be continued—

"La Llorona's Last Tear

or

Will 'Lowrider Sally Chingas' Rescue

Her Old Sidekick from Jefferson High and Save the Day?"

Subcomandante Chihuahua Speaks to the World Finance Ministers & the World Banko
4/12/00

Queridos Senyores:

Before I begin—
you may have seen me lately, in my usual beret camouflage of overexposure, "Latino" propaganda, and deconstructed flavor w/ an accent—these, as you know, have been my key strategies for simulated global satisfaction. Oh, excuse me, I am straying (like a good gato) from the subject at mano. It has come to my attention from various Chihuahua channels and dugouts south of the borderless and amorphous colonial zones (those multinational twin industry labor sites where the tiniest and most minute animalia dwell, either on lease to the Core Assembly Maquila or in SKID–containment centers [Silencing Krush Identification Deformation]) that we are just simply out of T.A.C.C.O. (Taut Automática Concentration Chamber Operas)! Yes, so it is. Therefore, as appointed representative for the CPC (Central Polysinew Committee—those few of us in charge of pulling the *P* out of the pully), I inform you that as of today (year of the cyber-perro) all Third World neighborhoods (where we are the majority) call for a T.A.C.C.O. strike to end world maquila hunger and world ambition. Please respond asap, with a memo from all the W-ministers. Upon receipt, you will be invited to a C.H.A.L.U.P.A. (Cease Heavy Absorption of Land Unilaterally & People's Autonomy) Roast for the World Banko. Come, come, por favor, join us in our new Chihuahua campaign for the twenty-first century to clear all Third World debts. Remember the Chihuahua motto: *If you wanna dog us, you gotta love us.*

book five

How to Make a Chile Verde Smuggler

Tía Lela and Juanito feeding the chickens on Juniper Street, Escondido, California, 1955

Interview at the Total Liberation Café

for La Maga

GODDESS: So, what did you say you do?

BOBO: Write, eat, work, write, you know.

GODDESS: Write? Why?

BOBO: So I can say something, come on, get with the program.

GODDESS: What about the pain?

BOBO: Did you say pain?

GODDESS: Read my lips—

BOBO: OK, OK—pain—so what, what do you want from me?

GODDESS: What about the pain?

BOBO: You asked that already.

GODDESS: See this scarred mountain to my left?

BOBO: Yeah, I see it, yeah—OK, so? Mountain—big deal.

GODDESS: It's the heat of sorrow in your heart.

BOBO: You gotta be kidding?

GODDESS: Where are you going, Bobo?

BOBO: What? What do you mean where am I going? Nowhere, I ain't in no
    big hurry. I don't know. Maybe downtown, hit the Red Log, listen to
    Selena—

GODDESS: Why are you choking your napkin?

BOBO: I'm writing down an idea.

GODDESS: There's nowhere to go, nothing to do or say.

BOBO: But—I want to say something, I don't know about you—

GODDESS: Wipe off the clown makeup, OK?

BOBO: What makeup? You on crack or what?

GODDESS: Let go of the mask, Bobo.

BOBO: Nobody tops what I do, baby. Call me what you like.

GODDESS: And the fire? Behind you?

BOBO: Oh, uh—that yellowish—uh—that funny flash under—

GODDESS: Your little habit—what do you call it?

BOBO: Come on, get serious, I'm clean. I don't even eat cow meat.

GODDESS: How can I say—the way your pinky wrenches the dark when you are asleep—your, uh—ambition?

BOBO: Look at you—what's with the turquoise Capezios? And—uh—what about that skinny muzzled lion under your feet? And—the seven daggers dangling from your heart and the liquid eye blinking from the center of your palm and the flying ancient faces dimming and melting on your canary muumuu, not to mention the laughing crucifix. I mean, come on—you want to talk about it?

GODDESS: You didn't mention the dark aged man curled up against the dust, wrapped in a rebozo. See the crooked leg shooting out of his mouth? How still he is? The rot pasted on his ass? Rags—so many rags. This man I carry on my back—you didn't mention him.

BOBO: Get off me. I was improvising.

GODDESS: Your father maybe—remember him? Your poems—the thing you call writing. How can I say—your shame. Capish?

BOBO: I am hungry.

GODDESS: I know. You're speechless.

BOBO: The universe sizzles in your throat and—

GODDESS: Then it gets lodged in your chest, it falls apart near your belly.

BOBO: All you have is this steely gray ache, spread out in a star shape—

GODDESS: From the center of your being forever flaming out into emptiness, and the silent explosions of rubbery naked stars—

BOBO: Drowning in the thick rush of a breath.

GODDESS: You lost it.

BOBO: Lost what?

GODDESS: Wake up, fool.

BOBO: I am awake, I've been awake since day one.

GODDESS: I said wake up—look around.

BOBO: There's nothing to see—just—anguish and geometry, Lorca said.

GODDESS: Stop it!

BOBO: What did you say?

GODDESS: I said stop it. I am leaving.

BOBO: Wait—what is that fancy green ring you're wearing?

GODDESS: Smoke, ashes, sand—ecstasy.

BOBO: Not that—this—tiny thread in the river.

GODDESS: Your hand touching my knee—how shall I say?—you.

BOBO: Ah.

How to Make a Chile Verde Smuggler
LAST CALL

I confess, I buried the chiles from Food City,
three blocks from Huerta Street—it was a father thing.
I remembered how he dragged his feet at the end,
how he made a leg out of 2×4's, how he carved a body
for himself, how the fire inside built him.
This was the secret—the fire inside.

You got me cold. See? Under the trunk.
Inside the extra-large plastic leather luggage, bloated.
Yeah, bloated with the goods. You can smell it
all the way from Old Mesilla. Buried it, I did.
One quick flash of the hands. It was a mother thing.

She blessed me one too many times.
She crossed her tiny hands over my face so.
I saw through the mountain furnace—this old road
of lives and cross blossoms and unturned stones.

The explosion was the secret.
The flavor, let's call it a flavor; it set out on its own.
So fast, so alive—it disappeared. Then,
I appeared.

Notebook Fragments

Abuelita Juanita, c. 1900

Tío Chente and Tío Beto, Fort Bliss, El Paso, Texas, 1920

The marriage of Juanita Martínez (right) and Alejo Quintana (seated), Mexico City, c. 1898

Tío Chente (standing right) and the Boys of Segundo Barrio, El Paso, Texas, c. 1923

About the Author

Juan Felipe Herrera has been a dishwasher, photographer, arts director, teatrista, antropoetista, Aztec dancer, graphic artist, cartoonist, salsa sauce specialist, actor, video artist, and stand-up comedian. A mostly vegetarian Capricorn, sign of the earth-rat, Free Tibet advocate, and Indian rights activist, he lives with his soul partner, Margarita Luna Robles, in Fresno, California, where he is a professor in the Department of Chicano and Latin American Studies at California State University, Fresno.

ML

10/02